EXTENDED PROJECT STUDENT COMPANION

- Extended Project Student Companion
- A student guide to support you through your EPQ

Lead Author Mary James

In association with

Gatsby Technical Education Projects
Nuffield Foundation Curriculum Programme

Great Clarendon Street, Oxford, OX2 6DP, United Kingdom

Oxford University Press is a department of the University of Oxford.
It furthers the University's objective of excellence in research, scholarship,
and education by publishing worldwide. Oxford is a registered trade mark of
Oxford University Press in the UK and in certain other countries

Text © Mary James 2009

The moral rights of the authors have been asserted

First published by Nelson Thornes Ltd in 2009
This edition published by Oxford University Press in 2014

All rights reserved. No part of this publication may be reproduced,
stored in a retrieval system, or transmitted, in any form or by any
means, without the prior permission in writing of Oxford University
Press, or as expressly permitted by law, by licence or under terms
agreed with the appropriate reprographics rights organization.
Enquiries concerning reproduction outside the scope of the above
should be sent to the Rights Department, Oxford University Press, at
the address above.

You must not circulate this work in any other form and you must
impose this same condition on any acquirer

British Library Cataloguing in Publication Data
Data available

978-1-4085-0408-6

10 9

Printed in Great Britain by CPI Group (UK) Ltd., Croydon CR0 4YY

Acknowledgements

Illustrations: Mark Draisey
Page make-up: Pantek Arts Ltd
Editors: Angela Hall and Jean Scrase
Advisers: Hilary Thomson and Nicola Wilberforce, Esher College; and Trevor Green

Although we have made every effort to trace and contact all
copyright holders before publication this has not been possible in all
cases. If notified, the publisher will rectify any errors or omissions at
the earliest opportunity.

Links to third party websites are provided by Oxford in good faith
and for information only. Oxford disclaims any responsibility for
the materials contained in any third party website referenced in
this work.

Contents

Introduction — 5
What is the EPQ, and how does it fit into my studies? — 5
The process involved in an EPQ — 7
How will my Extended Project be assessed? — 12
Checklist: are you ready to start your Extended Project? — 14

Chapter 1 Project management skills: starting out — 15

Choosing a topic — 16
What do we mean by 'extended'? — 16
Take a good hard look at yourself — 18
What constraints might affect your topic choice? — 19
Be inspired! – getting ideas to flow — 20
Building up an initial project idea — 22
Working as part of a group — 23
Working independently — 24
Checklist: are you ready for your initial planning meeting with your Supervisor? — 25
Initial planning for your project — 27
Project planning techniques — 30
Drawing up a detailed project plan — 31
Organisational skills – keeping your project on track — 32
Project proposal and approval — 34
Checklist: are you ready for your Project proposal meeting? — 35
Project progress checkpoint — 36

Chapter 2 Project management skills: researching the project — 37

Project management — 38
What sort of skills will I need to develop? — 39
Research methods — 42
Identifying likely resources — 43
Evaluating your resources — 44
Using the Internet effectively as a research tool — 48
Using people as subjects in your research — 50
Using questionnaires — 51
Reading strategies to help you gather relevant information quickly — 54
Representing information in your own way — 56
Using ICT to support your research — 56
Take good care of yourself — 56
Sorting and organising your data files — 59
Risk assessment — 61
Drawing up a risk assessment grid — 62

Contents

Skills to help your project run smoothly — 63
What do we mean by critical thinking? — 63
Statistics: strengths and weaknesses — 65
Decision making and problem solving skills — 68
Creative thinking — 71

Your mid-project review — 73
Remember the AQA EPQ Assessment Criteria — 74
Examples of students' work — 75
Planning your project product/artefact — 78

Checklist – are you ready for your mid-project review? — 79

Project progress checkpoint — 80

Chapter 3 Project management skills: producing the project product — 81

Report writing skills — 82
Selecting the presentation style of your report — 82
Using visuals in your report — 85
Defining your audience — 88
Think about the language of your report — 89
Manage the writing process — 90
Structuring your report — 91

Avoid plagiarism – get more marks for authenticity — 95

Referencing your sources — 97

Producing an artefact for your project product — 101
Selecting an appropriate product for your project — 101
AQA EPQ Assessment Criteria — 102

Checklist – are you ready for your end-of-project review? — 103

Project progress checkpoint — 104

Chapter 4 Presenting your project — 105

Different presentation styles: what should your presentation consist of? — 106

Presentation skills — 109
Using presentation software — 109
Communicating clearly — 111

Checklist – are you ready for your presentation and question and answer session? — 116

Project progress checkpoint — 118

Chapter 5 Finalising and submitting your project — 119

Evaluation and reflection — 120

Completing your Project Production Log — 122

Checklist – are you ready for your project submission? — 124

Project progress checkpoint — 126

Introduction

By the end of this section, you should:

- have a good idea of what the Extended Project Qualification (EPQ) is
- identify how you might benefit from and enjoy the EPQ
- understand what might be expected of you in an Extended Project
- confirm with your Supervisor that you want to be involved with the Extended Project.

What is the EPQ, and how does it fit into my studies?

The EPQ is an opportunity to do a project in a subject area in which you are interested. It provides a context for developing critical thinking and project management skills – these are widely transferable, and may be useful in other courses now or later on. The EPQ assesses your ability to plan, carry out, report on, and evaluate a project.

The emphasis of the assessment is on the process, a presentation and report, and other appropriate evidence of your work. It is a level 3 qualification which may be followed alongside other level 3 qualifications such as A levels, or may form part of a level 3 diploma.

The EPQ assesses your ability to plan, carry out, report on, and evaluate a project.

Introduction

EPQ as a free-standing qualification

Your Extended Project may be an extension to your GCE AS/A levels, BTEC, NVQ, or other academic or vocational qualification. It could be in an area these touch on, or could be quite different from your main subject areas.

Your Extended Project may be part of the AQA Baccalaureate (Bacc). The AQA Bacc has four elements:

- the recognised **academic study** of your main GCE A level choices
- **broader study** designed to develop your critical thinking and/or citizenship skills through the study of an AS level in General Studies, Citizenship or Critical Thinking
- **enrichment activities** which might be some specific community involvement (such as community work with a local charity), work-related learning, or personal development activities; these could be part of the Duke of Edinburgh Award scheme or your work in a debating society, for example
- **independent learning**: this is where your Extended Project comes in! Your Extended Project Qualification is part of the AQA Bacc.

EPQ as part of a Diploma course

If you are studying a Diploma qualification at level 3, then it is compulsory for you to follow the Extended Project. The Extended Project can complement or develop the Principal Learning, or extend other study areas or personal interests.

How is the EPQ different from my other studies?

There are certain requirements which set the Extended Project Qualification apart from your other studies, whether it is free-standing or part of a Diploma. There are five key principles which make the EPQ special.

- It requires **independent** research and learning to extend your studies.
- **You must choose** your path of study in negotiation with your Supervisor.
- You have to show that you can **plan, deliver and present** your project work.
- There is some teaching of necessary skills involved, but the majority of your learning will require your own **self motivation and strong organisational skills**.
- Your work will be monitored and 'mentored' by a **Project Supervisor**; they may suggest other people who can also help you.
- The EPQ will develop your independent research and study skills. You will learn how to carry out research effectively, and as you study something in more depth your personal, learning and thinking skills will improve.

Introduction

How will the Extended Project be of benefit to me?

The Extended Project should be enjoyable and fulfilling. It will also be challenging, so you need to have a clear idea of why you want to do the qualification. It brings you significant benefits.

- Completing the Extended Project will help you develop your own organisational, project management and independent learning skills. These skills will help you become a more confident student in other areas of study.
- The skills you develop as part of the Extended Project will provide you with a solid foundation in study and research skills. These skills will benefit you in your university studies, if you choose to go on to higher education, and in future employment.
- Being successful in the Extended Project Qualification is also likely to enhance your application to higher education. If you apply for a higher education course, the EPQ, will be recognised as half an A level or an essential part of the level 3 Diploma. It will help you to stand out from other students, both in your personal statement and at interview – this is particularly important when applying for popular university courses such as medicine and law, or if you are making an application to a top university.
- Because you are following an area of personal interest, the project will bring freshness to your studies, and might help you decide on future employment or educational options.

The process involved in an EPQ

What will I be required to do?

The AQA Extended Project Qualification[1], being recognised and formally accredited by Qualifications and Curriculum Authority (QCA), has specific requirements.

You will have to do the following:

1. Choose your topic or your area of interest that will form your individual project and submit this for formal approval.
2. Identify and draft the main aims and objectives of your project. Aims are broad, general statements about what you hope your project will achieve. Objectives are specific statements about what your project will cover. The objectives should contain action verbs such as 'identify', 'contrast', 'analyse', and 'construct'.
3. Plan, research and carry out your project. This will mean that you have to apply certain organisational skills and strategies to fulfil your objectives. You will also have to obtain and select information from a number of different sources, analyse your data and show that you understand the complexities of the topic you've chosen.
4. Provide evidence of all stages of your project process. There are certain essential requirements: you will, for example, have to complete a Production Log.
5. Produce a written report of between 1000 and 5000 words as part of your project product. (See page 12.)

---

[1] © AQA 2007 Please refer to the current version of the specification on AQA's website at www.aqa.org.uk/over/extendedproject.php.

6. Deliver a presentation about your project. You will need to present your project in a way that is appropriate for a non-specialist audience: this will be in a form that is appropriate for your chosen topic. You will be expected to respond to questions about your project.
7. Review and reflect on the whole project process.

You won't be doing this entirely on your own. You will have the help and support of a Project Supervisor who is based in your school/college – probably a teacher you know already, or another member of staff. You should also check the exact requirements of the project with a current version of the EPQ specification.

Key requirements

You must have all three of these to get a grade; production log, report, presentation (recording or other evidence that this has been done).

Will there be any teaching involved?

Completing the Extended Project Qualification will be more about learning than being taught, more about being guided in your studies than being set work. After all, it is looking to develop your independent research and learning skills. However there is a taught element, and your teachers will be able to give you more information on the form this will take in your school or college.

You will be supported by a **Supervisor** as you develop independent learning skills. Your supervisor will guide you, but you should take the lead.

It's likely, that although you and your peers will be doing very different topics, there will be some skills you can learn and develop as a group.

There is some generic information which is relevant for students carrying out projects. Here are some examples.

- There are accepted forms for academic writing which may be useful to you in structuring your written work. This will be important when you come to write up your report.
- Project management skills are needed, including how you manage your work within the time available, how you manage the resources you have access to, and how to search effectively for relevant information using libraries, the internet and other sources.
- How to carry out your project safely and effectively. If you are carrying out some work in a science laboratory, you will need to know about laboratory health & safety. For other types of research involving members of the public you may need to adhere to certain professional codes of conduct.

How will I work with my Supervisor?

Although there is a strong element of you as the learner working independently and taking responsibility for your own research, this high level of autonomy does not mean there will be no support on offer for you.

At your school or college, there will be a teacher or a member of staff who will be appointed as your Supervisor. Your Supervisor will support you along the journey from project proposal through to submission.

Introduction

Remember that there is a focus in the Assessment Objectives on the process, the evidence and your written report, rather than on the quality of the artefact itself.

Working with your Supervisor

At the very beginning of your project process, it would be useful for you to establish answers to the following questions with your Supervisor.

- How will you communicate? By email? Face-to-face? By phone?
- How often will you meet?
- Will you be able to contact your Supervisor during school/college holidays?
- If your Supervisor is not available, who should you discuss things with?
- How should you prepare for your face-to-face meetings?

Your Supervisor may or may not be a subject specialist in your area of research.
However they will be able to advise you on managing and developing your project. Remember, your presentation at the end of your project has to be aimed at a non-specialist audience.

Supervisor's responsibilities

The Supervisor's responsibilities will be, in broad terms, as shown in the table. Their main role is to guide you. You are responsible for owning your log and recording advice.

Project stage / book page no.	What your Supervisor will do	What AQA requires the Supervisor to do
Starting out on your project this book page 15	Agree the project proposal and the project title with you Meet with you to discuss how you intend to develop your initial idea into a full project	Complete the Supervisor's section of the **Project Proposal Form**
Researching your project this book page 37	Meet with you during your project to discuss progress	Conduct a mid-term review with you; they will record the advice and level of support offered throughout the project in your **Production Log**
Producing your project product this book page 81	Meet with you to discuss the project as it nears its end	Conduct an end-of-project review with you
Presenting your project this book page 107	Your Supervisor will be present at your presentation; they will ask you questions relating to your project and the presentation	Your Supervisor will have to confirm your presentation took place
Finalising and submitting your project this book page 119		Your Supervisor must endorse your **Production Log** and sign the front page
Assessing your project		The completed production log, the written report, the evidence and the presentation are assessed by your Supervisor

Can I work as part of a group?

You can work as a group, but be aware that you will each have to submit individual written reports detailing each person's contribution. You will each have to:

- create your own specific project proposal
- have your own particular focus or task within the group
- record your contributions and reflect on the work of the group.

You will be assessed as an individual, so your evidence must prove how you have met the Assessment Objectives (see pages 40–41) and performance criteria.

Introduction

What others might do to support you

Librarians, in your school or college library or local public library, could help you with your research, by advising you on the availability of resources. You will be assessed on how well you obtain and select information from a variety of sources, so it's important that you explore all relevant options.

There may be other people whose skills and experience you can draw on and who may be very keen to help:

- your parents/guardians
- local employers or local business–education partnerships
- local universities and colleges
- local museums, galleries, theatres and other community organisations
- professional organisations and societies
- members of staff within your school or college who have interests or recent research experience in your topic area.

You don't have to feel that independent learning is working alone. There are plenty of people who can advise and support you, and above all, you can always talk to your Supervisor.

Using this book

This book gives guidance on the journey you make whilst identifying, researching, and presenting your project and during the report writing phase. It is full of tips and techniques to help you develop and practise the skills required to carry out your project work successfully. Each phase has been carefully broken down.

- This book introduces you to the skills required during each phase, and explains how they will be important to your project work.
- It provides brief activities to help you learn, practise and apply the relevant skill.
- 'What this means to my project' helps you apply this learning to your individual project.
- 'Study Tips' help demystify the marking process and show where you could lose marks.
- 'Key Terms' highlight and explain important words or phrases.
- 'Checklists' help prepare you for meetings with your project Supervisor.
- 'Project Progress Checkpoints' highlight exactly what stage you are at in your project, and how it fits into the whole process. These will prompt you to make sure you are ready for the next stage of your project process.

Much of this information about generic skills will be useful to any student doing EPQ. Your Supervisor can also give you the more subject-specific material available in the Supervisor Support Pack.

How will my Extended Project be assessed?

See the table on the next pages.

What AQA require

Four elements of your Extended Project are required as assessment evidence for AQA. Always check the most recent version of the specifications, as changes are made from time to time.

1 The completed Production Log

Every student enrolled for this qualification has an AQA Production Log. It provides AQA with a documented record of the journey of your project. It is your responsibility to make sure that every element is complete.

2 Appropriate evidence of your project

This evidence is likely to have different forms, depending on the topic or the nature of your subject area. It may be for example:

- an artefact or a photographic record for a creative arts project
- a performance or recording for a performing arts project
- a prototype or model
- a slide or PowerPoint presentation
- a computer program.

These forms of evidence may not be necessary if you choose the format of the longer 5000 word report.

3 A written report

All students must provide a **written report**. The length of the report will depend on the nature of your project. If most of your project work involves the production of an artefact or product (as listed above), then your written report will be a minimum of 1000 words and will be a record of the work you undertook. Remember that you will be assessed on the process and the report rather than the product itself. If your project is made up entirely of written work, such as an exploration of a theory, then it should be longer, at approximately 5000 words.

4 A presentation

This may be a written or oral presentation, and should use the most appropriate medium for your project and audience. This may include PowerPoint slides, a performance, photographs, videos or an exhibition. Whichever form your report presentation takes, you will be expected to respond to questioning.

You must provide written evidence of your presentation having taken place.

Introduction

How will my Extended Project be assessed?

Project stage / book page no.	What you will do	What AQA requires you to do
Starting out on your project *this book page 15*	Select your topic/area of interest Decide on a project outline and the main objective of your project Plan your project so as to meet the initial objective Agree the project title with your Supervisor	Complete the **Project Proposal Form** in the **Production Log**
Researching your project *this book page 37*	Conduct the research that your project plan requires Record your research and the resources that you make use of Meet with your Supervisor, record any action you take as a result of their advice or guidance Record any changes you make to your plan and why you have decided to make these changes	Record the research in your **Production Log** and how your work relates to your main areas of study
Producing your project product *this book page 89*	Produce the project report, evidence and any artefact	Provide **appropriate evidence** to support your project. This may take a variety of forms All students must provide a **written report** of between 1000-5000 words. The length of this report will relate to the nature of your project (see page 12)
Presenting your project *this book page 105*	Share your project with others, using a format and media that is relevant to your project Be prepared to answer questions about your project after this presentation	Deliver your presentation, targeted at a non-specialist audience. Your presentation needs to be recorded in the **Production Log**, and your Supervisor must confirm in the log that it has taken place
Reviewing finalising and submitting your project *this book page 119*	Reflect on the process of producing your project	Complete your **Production Log**, ensuring that it includes your reflections on the process of your project

Introduction

Checklist: are you ready to start your Extended Project?

Your Extended Project should be a very rewarding and exciting educational experience. You will be expected to work independently and develop new skills, but you will have plenty of support through your project Supervisor and by using this resource.

Before starting on your Extended Project, make sure you are appropriately prepared for what it will involve. Make notes on the following[1].

	My response …
The benefits to me of carrying out an Extended Project are …	
The implications of committing my time and resource to the Extended Project are …	
The following teachers/tutors are happy to provide me with appropriate support …	
I think that a topic for a good Extended Project could be …	
I will ensure that my Extended Project has an equal focus on both the project content and its process by …	
The time I have available to research my project and complete it appropriately is …	
Having thought about it, I am likely to work on a project as part of a group / to create an individual piece of work because…	
What else do I need to do? (such as people to talk to, and research on possible topics)	

〉〉〉〉〉〉〉〉 *Next steps*

You will be required to identify the topic for your project and to explore the possible aims and objectives. See the next chapter of this book.

---

[1]Filling in this chart is not an AQA requirement for your EPQ. However it may help you to prepare for a meeting with your Supervisor.

Project management skills: starting out

Getting started on your Extended Project will be an exciting time, allowing you some real independence in a chosen topic area that is likely to motivate and inspire you. Don't let that enthusiasm to 'get into it' stop you from taking time and effort to carefully plot your journey and identify your ultimate goals. It will help you succeed if you establish the aims for your project at the start, and make sure your project plan makes appropriate use of both time and available resources.

You might want to complete your EPQ in conjunction with work experience or some other activity, as long as this provides scope for you to cover the assessment requirements.

This chapter will help you to:

- think about the factors governing your choice of topic for the EPQ
- practise some techniques to determine your choice of topic
- identify whether you will work on your own or as part of a group
- establish your project aims and objectives
- plan your project and explore the issues that will help you achieve your goals
- fulfil the requirements of AQA's project approval process.

Your supervisor will support you

Choosing a topic

By the end of this section, you should be able to:
- explore the factors which might affect your topic choice
- understand what we mean by 'extended' and how that will help you make your topic choice
- identify your project aims and objectives
- prepare for your initial planning meeting with your Project Supervisor.

What do we mean by 'extended'?

The 'extended' nature of the EPQ is what makes it a unique qualification at this level. It is that which sets it apart from anything you are likely to have done to date in your studies. You have to make sure that your project matches this expectation.

- It is a single and original piece of work.
- It requires good quality planning and preparation.
- It requires you to use a high degree of independence in your research.
- It allows you to go beyond the rigid structure of a single specification or subject area.
- It allows you to make links between topics or within subject areas in a way that your current timetable doesn't cater for.

This means that you will be developing and extending a specific area of your studies, or a personal interest or activity, in such a way that your final project topic would not normally fall within your main programme of study.

So what does this mean in practice?

- **You can't resubmit a piece of work that you have already completed as part of another examination.**
- **You can't reuse a project that you had already completed as part of another course of study.**

Chapter 1: Project management skills: starting out

An Extended Project encourages real creativity, independent exploration, innovation, and to some extent, risk-taking. These will extend your own knowledge, skills and experience and underpin your development as a researcher.

Bear in mind this quotation from the eminent scientist, Albert Einstein, who developed the theory of relativity:

'If we knew what we were doing it wouldn't be research, would it?'

What does this mean in terms of level?

In terms of the level required, an Extended Project Qualification is a level 3 qualification, equivalent to A level. You may be doing it alongside your AS levels, so have not necessarily reached an A level standard in other subject areas yet. To achieve this qualification, your work must reach the same level as an A level.

We've talked about the EPQ being the equivalent of an AS level. To be clear about this.

- The planning, research, execution and presentation of your project must reflect an A level (A2) standard (so could be awarded an A*).
- The qualification is worth the same number of UCAS points as an AS level.

When choosing the topic area for your research, it might be difficult to decide where to begin. Consider the questions on the next page – these might help lead you to your chosen area.

Key term

Extended Your project must develop skills, knowledge and experience outside your main programme of study to an A level or level 3 standard.

Take a good hard look at yourself

ACTIVITY Look at yourself

1. Think carefully about the following questions. These should prompt some thinking around topic areas that would reflect your skills, experience and personal interests.

    A Which subject areas have you enjoyed?
    (This might not be the same as those areas you know you are good at.)

    B Which activities do you describe yourself as passionate about?

    C Of the following skills, which ones would you mark yourself with 7/10 or more?

    - skim-reading for an overview of text
    - putting people at ease and getting them to talk
    - creative writing
    - analysing information
    - getting the most out of IT
    - performing in front of an audience
    - making products

    D Is there a topic or subject area you have always wanted to find out more about?

    E If you are thinking of going to university or starting employment, is there a topic relevant to this?

    F When you first thought about doing an EPQ, what was your first thought as to a suitable project? Gut instinct is often right! If there is an idea that keeps nagging away at you, go back to it.

Enjoy it!

Whatever you decide to do, and whatever format your final project presentation takes, make sure you enjoy it! Most worthwhile ventures are hard work, so you might be more successful if you are motivated by a project you can get passionate about.

Chapter 1: Project management skills: starting out

What constraints might affect your topic choice?

Doing something you enjoy might provide lots of positive thinking and optimism, but you'll still need to keep your feet on the ground. Several factors might restrict your project choice.

ACTIVITY Constraints

1. Consider the following questions. These may show some obstacles to your choice of topic area. You may want to make some notes, and discuss your answers with your Project Supervisor.

   A Has your school/college laid down any expectations? Do they expect you to work within a particular department or faculty which might determine the subject area?

   B Does your school/college expect you to combine certain AS or A level subjects and to steer your choice along a particular area of study?

   C Is there an examination requirement that your project reflects a particular line of learning, or where your project has to complement other subject areas?

   D Have you been told that you can or can't make use of specialist accommodation or equipment? Do you need natural light or dark room facilities? Do you have to work within a specific space? (It's no good trying to create a large sculpture if you only have a cupboard to work in.)

   E Are you required to work with a partner or as part of a group? This might be so where your project is performance-related, requiring several different roles; or an engineering project which requires you to be working as part of a team.

   F Do you need to keep it in line with diploma requirements?

Study tip Even if you are working as part of a group, you must make sure that you have an identifiable role or input which can be assessed as your contribution to the group project.

Link

For more information on working as part of a group, go to page 23.

Be inspired! – getting ideas to flow

People can be inspired in different ways. Some learners work hard whilst others sit back and seemingly wait for an idea to hit them. There are several techniques you can use to build up some original ideas for a project topic. You might use a spidergram, generating ideas (either on your own or in a group), or an ideas grid. Ideas will come more easily once you start paying attention to them and start to nurture them.

Building up a spidergram

Start with a theme and write that down in the middle of a piece of paper. Relax, be open to ideas and just write down whatever that theme suggests to you. Don't reject anything you think of – note each point down as it occurs to you and allow it to connect in some way to the next. There are no right or wrong ideas – you just need to write something down and then let your mind think of the next idea. You could then circle the most relevant themes and create a new spidergram from each of those.

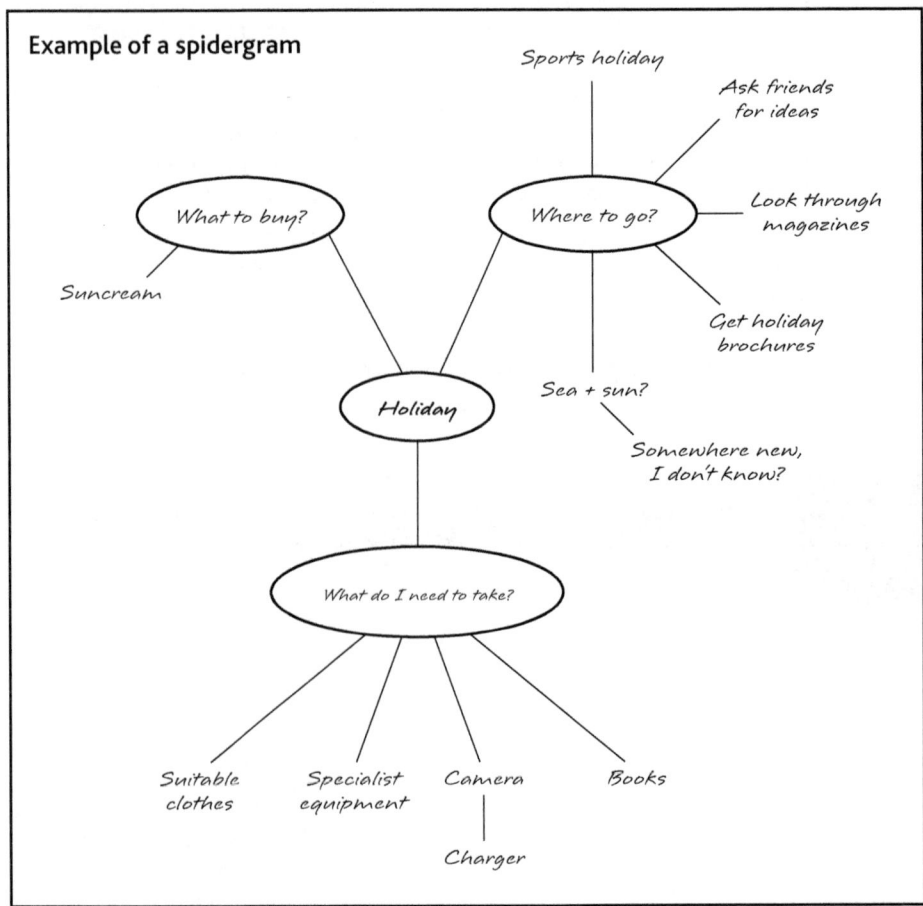

Ideas grid
This is often used for generating ideas for a story line or plot for a performance-based project.
1. Create a grid with appropriate headings in each column.
2. Working one column at a time, note every single idea that might work under that heading. For example, for genre, you could list romance, comedy, and tragedy.
3. Cover your first column and then note down some possibilities for the second column. For example, at a computer, in a bus, or at a seaside resort.
4. You can then do the same for the third column and so on.
5. Once you have completed the grid, you look across the columns, matching up different combinations to create the beginnings of a storyline.

Genre	Setting	Theme/key event	Main character	Other characters
Romance	At a computer	War and peace	Time traveller	Baby
Comedy	In a bus	Generation gap	Lone dad	Metallurgist
Tragedy	At a seaside resort	Managing capitalism	Olympic hero	Charity worker
Fantasy	Singapore shopping mall	Long term illness	Medical student	Journalist

Ideas shower: generating ideas
Everyone needs to be clear about the rules for generating ideas. To be successful, an ideas shower session has to be structured.
- Start with a goal: set yourself an objective for your session.
- Time your session, about 10-20 minutes. If you need to re-start, have an break first.
- Generate ideas in a place where you know you will be relaxed, somewhere you don't normally work.
- Always have a pen and paper, a flip chart or a whiteboard to jot down all your ideas. A group may have a scribe whose only role is to record the ideas.
- Note every idea that comes into your head: nothing is too stupid to include. In fact, something may initially sound silly but lead onto something good.

Building up an initial project idea

You have by now a much better idea of the topic **area** for your project. You need to identify the initial idea, and to clarify the planned path or aims and objectives. This path requires you to identify either:

- a '**working title**' if the end product is a report

or

- a '**working objective**' if the end product is an artefact (such as a piece of art or software program) or an event (such as a performance).

Identify your project's aims and objectives

Your working title or objective must have a clear focus. You will present it as part of the Project Proposal Form and give it a title. This title should be a single phrase presenting the topic succinctly and clearly. It may be a short statement, a question, or a hypothesis. Any one of these may look to solve a problem, seek to confirm or deny a theory, or suggest an investigation to explore an issue. Previous examples of titles have included:

- Concrete or asphalt for motorway surfaces?
- Design and make a dress inspired by the development of women's freedom from society's restraints.
- To what extent has the economic development of Mauritius aided the government in meeting its economic objectives?
- How has English affected the German language? Is this leading to its decline as a world language?
- Is the banning of plastic bags in Lyme Regis making Lyme Bay a greener place?

Your aims and objectives will include your **proposed action**, that is, the key tasks you consider necessary to fulfil the project outline as well as the format for the presentation for your project.

Can you explain your project to others? Share your project title, aims and objectives with another student. You are well on the way if you can explain why you are carrying out this project, what it will be called, and what you hope to achieve in terms of products and outcomes.

Key terms

Product This is the item you create. It is an AQA requirement, along with your Production Log and your presentation. It may be an extended essay/report, an event or an artefact.

Artefact This is a generic term given to a range of products that are created, invented or developed as part of or as a result of your project.

Chapter 1: Project management skills: starting out

■ Working as part of a group

If you are working as part of a group, because either you've been advised to or you have chosen to, there are several factors you need to consider in order to meet the AQA assessment requirements. The qualification is awarded to an individual so moderators need to be able to assess your individual contribution. Your group project might involve, for example, creating a group project product, such as a performance, show, exhibition or conference, but you must make a distinct element (contribution) that can be identified as yours.

What this means for my project

- ✓ Discuss your individual contribution with your Supervisor at an early stage.
- ✓ You will have to submit individual reports as part of your project which detail your own contribution.
- ✓ The evidence you submit will have to show that you personally have met all the Assessment Objectives and performance criteria.
- ✓ You may each have different aims and objectives although it is part of a group project.
- ✗ You can't all submit the same report: that wouldn't represent an individual's work.
- ✗ It is unlikely that you will all be working to the same aims and objectives, even if you have the same group project.
- ✗ You can't all perform the same role within a group project.
- ✗ You can't replicate the same sections from one report in someone else's.
- ✗ You can't submit work that has already been submitted as a coursework element on a different qualification.

Study tip

Extended: Your project has to build on or extend knowledge, skills or experience within a specific topic area and not duplicate work that has previously been set or submitted for another qualification.

Working independently

Completing your Extended Project gives you the opportunity to choose your own topic of study and work on your own. This is great preparation for employment or higher education. It may also be one of the first times where you've had to take responsibility for your own work to this degree.

ACTIVITY Independent working

1. Independent working has its own risks. Read the statements A–E below, then decide your level of experience of these risk factors (where 1 = no experience at all; 2 = some experience, and 3 = lots of experience). On the right, write a number 1–3 and note how you intend to overcome these risk factors.

   A believing you have lots more time than you do, particularly at the start

   B not structuring and planning your time in detail

   C missing key deadlines

   D not giving yourself key deadlines, or monitoring your progress against your plan

   E not asking for advice and support from the right people

Study tip

Working independently does not mean you are on your own. Your Project Supervisor will schedule key meetings with you, and will be available at other times to offer advice, guidance and support. If your Supervisor can't help you, they'll be able to suggest other people who can.

Chapter 1: Project management skills: starting out

Checklist: are you ready for your initial planning meeting with your Supervisor?

As part of your extended project, you are required to gain AQA approval for your project title. Your Supervisor will discuss with you exactly how to go about getting your project approved. Work through your initial idea with your Supervisor to get some early feedback.

> **Study tip**
>
> Make sure you can 'sell' your project idea to your Supervisor. Practise describing it in one or two sentences so that it sounds succinct and clear. If you can convince yourself that it's something you are passionate about and that it will encourage you to work in sufficient depth (that is at A2 level/level 3 standard), your Supervisor will recognise this and be better equipped to help you gain approval.

Validating your project idea means asking yourself some tough questions. You need to be sure that your idea has sufficient potential for you to gain the highest marks. Use this checklist to make sure you're prepared to meet your Supervisor[1].

	Yes	No	If no, why not? Comment on your next steps
I have a clear idea of how completing an EPQ will be of benefit to me			
I have carefully considered the time I need to make available for completing my Extended Project			
I have thought carefully about my topic area and know it really interests me			
I have considered what restrictions I have in terms of the resources and space available to me and to what extent this impacts on my topic choice			

Chart continued overleaf

---

[1]Filling in this chart is not an AQA requirement for your EPQ. However it may help you to prepare for a meeting with your Supervisor.

Chapter 1: Project management skills: starting out

	Yes	No	If no, why not? Comment on your next steps
I have given sufficient thought to my project title and feel confident it will give me scope to fulfil the AQA assessment criteria			
I have a good idea of the financial costs involved with carrying out my project and have considered if this affects my topic choice			
I've drawn up a draft project title			
I've got a good idea of my project aims and objectives			
My project title allows me to make use of high-level research skills including planning, analysis, evaluation and explanation			
(If working as part of a group) I know that my contribution is entirely unique within the group: no other group member has the same aims and objectives			
The questions I need to ask my Supervisor in my initial planning meeting are:			
As a result of my meeting with my Project Supervisor, I need to:			

Chapter 1: Project management skills: starting out

Initial planning for your project

By the end of this section, you should be able to:

- explore the tasks and sub-tasks involved in the work of your project
- identify the timings involved in each phase of the project
- understand a variety of project planning techniques available to you
- draft an initial plan for your project.

Project planning

A project is more likely to be worthwhile and successful if you do some research before you start. You need to identify the sort of tasks you need to do, and whom or where you will consult in order to fulfil your objectives. This planning process will allow you to anticipate the risks involved and the problems you might face, and to manage your project efficiently.

Project planning techniques are useful in many different situations, such as planning a holiday, a gap year, a revision programme or a work-related task. A thorough plan helps you to make sure that your goals are achievable within the time and budget you have available.

> **Study tip**
>
> The most common comment offered by students when they reflect on the work of their Extended Project is:
>
> *'If I did this again I would plan my time better.'*

What factors do you need to consider?

Several different factors will impact on the successful completion of your project. These might include the following.

- **Time available**: work back from your final deadline, and include any interim dates you need to meet. Also consider other commitments in and out of college, and deadlines for other courses you are doing. What time do you have to dedicate to the required tasks? How much time will each task take? To keep yourself on track, break your project into a series of phases with short-term deadlines.
- **Resources available**: what specialist equipment or materials will be needed? Are these all readily available, or do you need to find them yourself?

> **Key Term**
>
> **Project plan** this is a project timeline which details the key tasks and major milestones you need to achieve to fulfil your project.

- **Dependencies**: work out the sequence of tasks to be carried out. Note which tasks can only be done once a preceding task has been completed. This is the **critical path** of your project plan. It highlights the items in your schedule which could hold up the remaining phases of the project. For example, you can't hold an event such as a football match unless you have found somewhere to play. The stage when other tasks are done may not be critical to the success of the project.
- **Risks or potential problems**: what could go wrong? Might problems get in your way? Does your plan rely too heavily on a busy person's contribution? Do you need some 'buffer' time or contingency, in case problems arise?

Checklist for successful project planning

Clear goals: write down exactly what it is you are hoping to achieve.

Communication: work out how and when you will communicate with other people involved in or interested in your project's progress.

Risk management: anticipate the potential problems and create a 'Plan B' should these occur.

Keep realistic: be entirely realistic about the resources you have: stay rational and down-to-earth about the schedule and scope of the project.

Keep on track: identify exactly how you will keep to the deadlines you have set yourself, and monitor your own progress.

Clearly define roles and responsibilities: if you're working as part of a group, make sure everyone involved in your project is clear about what, how and when they should do their tasks.

Making a diary

Making a diary is essential to planning your own time, keeping you on track, and reducing the risks of working independently.

- ✓ Many students choose a 'week to a view' diary.
- ✓ At the start, write in all your appointments with your Project Supervisor.
- ✓ Write in your key project dates as outlined in your own project plan.
- ✓ Include all the AQA deadlines (available online, and your Supervisor will know them).
- ✓ Add other activities in your project plan, showing when they have to be done and completed.
- ✓ Plan time for fun and rest as well!
- ✓ Keep your diary with you always – and refer to it regularly.
- ✓ Phone-based or online calendars, such as those in email software, would also enable you to set up dates and email reminders.

Chapter 1: Project management skills: starting out

For project planning techniques see pages 30–31.

 ACTIVITY Project planning

As part of a school charity day, there will be a music stall selling second-hand music related items (including CDs, mp3 players, instruments, books). You have been tasked with producing the promotional leaflet to market the event around the school. With a budget of £50 you have to produce 200 leaflets to distribute in the staff room, classrooms, the library, and so on. You have three weeks to fulfil the brief.

Using one of the project planning techniques described overleaf, or one of your own:

1 Break down this project into smaller tasks and estimate the time needed for each task.

2 Identify the dependencies – that is which tasks can only be done when another has been completed.

3 Prepare a project plan.

4 Is it all manageable within the time and money resources you have available? If not, what changes do you need to make?

What this means for my project

This type of project planning is vital for the successful development of your Extended Project. At the same time, your Project Proposal Form requires you to list elements that you will establish as part of the project planning process. On the form, you need to list:

- the research/activity/task to be carried out
- the sources you will consult in your research (these might involve you accessing library resources, the Internet, or carrying out some face to face interviews)
- your proposed actions.

Study tip

Your Project Proposal Form requires you to list any likely resources you will make use of in your project work. It's helpful, therefore, to make a note of any books, websites, data or evidence you refer to in your initial planning which may be relevant for your project. This represents good practice for when you move on to your full research anyway.

Project planning techniques

There are a several project planning tools and techniques you can use.

Planning with Gantt charts

A Gantt chart is a useful tool to help schedule actions and tasks which are part of a project that has a number of stages. A Gantt chart is a horizontal bar chart showing the scheduled tasks and dependencies against a timeline. It will:

- ✓ help you to break down tasks into smaller chunks of work
- ✓ assist in working out a critical path for a project
- ✓ help you to plan for periods of more intense activity
- ✓ help you to monitor progress and check whether you are on schedule or not.

To create a Gantt chart

1. Make a list of all the activities you think will form part of the project you need to plan. Be as comprehensive as you can.
2. List the length of time you think each task should take. Work out which tasks must precede (come before) others, and which tasks can be done in parallel.
3. On a piece of graph paper (or you might choose to use spreadsheet software), list the days/weeks/months you have available to complete your project across the horizontal (*x*) axis.
4. Down the vertical (*y*)axis, list all the activities in the correct order of completion. Then draw a horizontal bar beside each task to represent the length of time it will take.

Planning with sticky notes

This can be a very practical way to visualise the tasks you have ahead. You can do this as a team if you are working as part of a group, or you can do it on your own.

1. List all the tasks and sub-tasks that make up your project and write each one of them on a sticky note. At this point, you just need to list everything. Don't worry about getting them in the right order.
2. Now group the sticky notes together into larger areas of activity. Write how long each task should take on each sticky note.
3. On a whiteboard, create a start point on the left and an end point on the right. Place the sticky notes in a logical line, drawing a line into each activity box (or sticky note) and a line out. This will help you identify dependencies.

Using online planning templates

You can also find free planning templates online; these provide a structure which you can personalise for your own needs.

Chapter 1: Project management skills: starting out

■ Drawing up a detailed project plan

Having looked at the different project planning techniques available to you, you should now be able to consider your own project in more detail and create your own project plan.

Your plan

Your plan will need to detail the following.

1. **Main tasks** involved in carrying out your project.
2. **Sub-tasks** related to these main tasks.
3. **Critical path** of your project: what are the dependencies? This means you need to think about which tasks can only be done once something else has been done first. For example, are there particular materials you need to get hold of before starting work?
4. **Time you have available:** the deadline for submission, as well as interim project approval dates and so on, are laid down by AQA; your school/college may also make deadline requirements of you.
5. **Time that each task and sub-task will take.**
6. **Risks** that might be involved during your project, together with a plan of action should they materialise.
7. **Budget** (if applicable) that you are working to.
8. **Who** you will be working with (if anyone);
9. How often will you communicate/meet up with your Project Supervisor?
10. **Format** you have decided is best to present your project.
11. **How you will monitor your own progress** against the project plan. This is a very important part of your project plan and should include all relevant details. For example, what sort of checks will you put in place to ensure that you're on target to achieve your objectives? How will you know that each element of your project is being given the appropriate amount of time, and that you will finish it on schedule? If you have to divert from the original plan, perhaps for good reason, what will you do?

ACTIVITY Drawing up a plan

Using one of the techniques described above, draw up an initial plan for your own Extended Project.

Study tip

You are more likely to achieve the highest marks if you have a detailed project plan, and can provide clear evidence of how you will monitor your progress against the agreed project plan, even if you later change this plan. You will achieve lower marks if your project plan is brief, with little evidence of how you will keep track of your project's development.

Organisational skills – keeping your project on track

Of course, coming up with a good project plan is not all of it. It's a great start – and absolutely essential. You've also got to keep track of progress and ensure you're on schedule to succeed.

ACTIVITY Personal organisational skills audit

1. Identify a project or a task you completed recently. It may be related to school work, part time work, or something in your free time. Write down what it was.

   A Make a note of all the skills you used **really well** to carry out this task.

   B Make a note of all the skills you **could have improved** in order to do this task better.

2. Define the organisational skills you believe are necessary for successful completion of your project. Write these down, dividing up your ideas into:

   A those which are a 'must-have' or essential

   B those which are a 'nice to have' or desirable

ACTIVITY Matching competencies and skills requirements

1. How do your own competencies match up to the skills requirements listed on page 33? Decide what level of experience you have in these areas. Write a number 1–3 beside each list item, according to the following levels:

   A no experience at all = 1

   B some experience = 2

   C lots of experience = 3

2. In the areas where you have no experience or very little, consider what you will do to compensate for this or how you will work differently with regard to your Extended Project. Your Supervisor might be able to help here.

Chapter 1: Project management skills: starting out

Organisational skills for the purposes of your Extended Project involve three key areas.

Managing your time
We often hear the phrase 'time management', but we can't manage time, only the activities we do within that time.

✓ Plan out each task and sub task to be completed by a particular date.

✓ Plan your time so that you know exactly when you will be working on your Extended Project.

✓ Protect this planned time carefully.

✓ Carry out tasks in the most effective order, and always be aware of the critical path of your project.

Managing yourself

✓ Start with a positive commitment to fulfil your Extended Project.

✓ Challenge your own tendency to get distracted – developing self-discipline is crucial.

✓ List the tasks you will do at the beginning of each planned period of work; short term goals are as important as long term goals.

✓ Learn to adjust or amend your plans as required.

✓ Build in rewards for completing some of your goals.

Managing your environment

✓ Re-adjust others' expectations of you and what free time you will have available.

✓ Identify where you work best, both at school/college and at home.

✓ Organise your desk so that you are working most effectively.

✓ Organise your files on your computer and regularly make a back up of all your work.

✓ Make your notes on A4 punched paper so you can easily file them in a ring binder and organise/index them appropriately.

✓ User a planner, diary or calendar to assign time to tasks.

Project proposal and approval

By the end of this section, you should:

- understand what is involved in the project approval process and why it matters
- appreciate what your Project Supervisor needs to consider when assessing your project idea
- be able to prepare for your Project proposal meeting with your Project Supervisor.

What is involved in the project approval process?

AQA has a formal project approval process which you need to be aware of. This process helps you and your Supervisor make sure that you have chosen an appropriate area of study and project objectives. This is a check that you will be able to fulfil the assessment criteria and achieve success. Your Project Supervisor will support you through this process, but it is important that you understand the requirements. See the AQA specification[1].

Checklist for the approval of titles

Your Supervisor will need to check the following:

✓ Your project topic allows for the **development and extension** of your skills and knowledge outside of your main areas of study, or **develops/complements your principal learning** as part of the Diploma.

✓ Your project allows you to access the **higher level concepts and skills in the assessment objectives**, that is that you can plan, research, analyse, evaluate, and explain – rather than simply describe and narrate.

✓ Your project title is **clear and focussed** on a specific issue which will allow you to fulfil it within the timescale and within the word limits, and that it will not end up either too long or too short.

✓ Your project title will allow you to **work independently**, investigating and researching your objectives without having to rely on a very small number of existing resources which would limit the potential for original work.

✓ You will be able to approach your project **impartially** and in an entirely balanced way.

✓ You have a good idea of the **format and date of presentation** of your final project.

✓ If you are working as part of a group, your **own individual contribution** is carefully defined.

---

[1] © AQA, 2007 Please refer to the current version of the specification on AQA's website at www.aqa.org.uk/over/extendedproject.php.

Chapter 1: Project management skills: starting out

Checklist: are you ready for your Project Proposal meeting?

Use this checklist to make sure you're appropriately prepared[1].

	My notes
I have carefully considered which topic area I'd like to form the basis of my research, and it is …	
My project title is …	
The way this project allows me to fulfil the assessment criteria is …	
The way I will monitor my progress against my project plan is …	
I have carried out a skills audit and the risks involved in organising my project and available time are …	
I will manage time and resources as part of my project plan by …	
The issues involved with working independently are…	
The time I have available is …	
The questions to ask my Project Supervisor in my Project Proposal meeting are…	
What else do I need to do?	

What this means for my project

The work of this chapter allows you and your Project Supervisor to complete parts A and B of the AQA Project Proposal Form. Your Supervisor may choose to complete part B during your Project proposal meeting. Completed Parts A and B of the Project Proposal Form form part of the evidence required for assessment and moderation.

---

[1] Filling in this chart is not an AQA requirement for your EPQ. However it may help you to prepare for a meeting with your Supervisor.

Chapter 1: Project management skills: starting out

Project progress checkpoint

▼ 1 Project management skills: starting out

Have you completed section A of the Project Proposal Form?	Yes	No
Have you discussed the Project Proposal Form, and in particular, section B of the Form with your Supervisor?	Yes	No
Have you got all the information you need regarding the approval process within your own centre?	Yes	No

▶ 2 Project management skills: researching the project

▶ 3 Project management skills: producing the project product

▶ 4 Presenting your project

▶ 5 Finalising and submitting your project

>>>>>>>> *Next steps*

The next stage of your Extended Project Qualification is to start on the research for your project. As a result of your discussion with your Project Supervisor, you might choose to make amendments or changes to your project plan. This will involve using resources effectively, and the development of skills such as critical thinking, decision making, and problem solving to support you in the successful completion of this stage.

Project management skills: researching the project

2

Now you have an approved project title and a plan, you need to start researching information and developing new skills. Skills and techniques may be introduced as part of the taught element of the EPQ course. The skills introduced in this chapter are likely to be useful to most students – you should take the opportunity to understand and apply them whatever the subject area of your project.

This chapter will help you to:

- refine your project plan in the light of your Project proposal meeting
- apply different research techniques and use resources effectively
- reference resources appropriately in line with academic protocols
- use the Internet effectively as a research tool
- use ICT appropriately to support and benefit your research
- prepare for your mid-project review.

Staying still gets you nowhere.

Chapter 2: Project management skills: researching the project

Project management

By the end of this section, you should be able to:

- review your project plan having met with your Supervisor
- link your project work, including the development of new skills, to EPQ assessment criteria.

Review your project plan

As a result of discussions with your Project Supervisor at your Project proposal meeting, you may now wish to revise your plan.

Remember that planning is a key part of the success of your Extended Project Qualification and you will be given credit for this. You should avoid rushing into the research and final production without being clear about your plan.

You should also think about the research methods you are going to use – see page 42.

> **Study tip**
>
> You should now complete page 8 of the AQA Candidate Record Form where you need to detail any changes, clarifications or additions as a result of advice from your Project Supervisor and Centre Coordinator.

Chapter 2: Project management skills: researching the project

What sort of skills will I need to develop?

Part of your Extended Project Qualification will be delivered in class time, although individual centres decide exactly what is taught and how they timetable this. Most centres will devote about 30 hours of teaching time to introduce you to skills that are useful to *most* students. If you need additional specialist skills, then your Project Supervisor will advise you on the best way to go about developing these skills.

Note that you will be assessed on the evidence you can provide of the skills you have developed. In the AQA EPQ assessment criteria[1].

- **Twenty per cent (20%) of the marks** are for how well you identify, design, plan, and complete the individual project or task within a group project and how well you **manage your project**.
- **A further 20% of the marks** available relate to your **use of resources and your research**. You will have to obtain and select information from a range of sources, analyse data, apply it relevantly and demonstrate understanding of any appropriate linkages, connections and complexities in your topic.
- **Forty per cent (40%) of the marks** are for how well you **make decisions, problem solve and think creatively** to achieve your outcomes.
- **Finally, 20% of the marks** are allocated to how well you **evaluate your learning and communicate your findings**.

Not all the skills you are taught will be immediately relevant. The ability to reflect on what you have learned, then select and apply the skills needed for your project, is critical to a successful EPQ student.

The Assessment Objectives table on the next pages shows how individual skills are assessed, and how you can gain marks for these skills.

> **Key term**
>
> **Reflection on your learning**
> Careful thought and consideration of what you are taught, and deciding if it is useful or relevant to your needs.

---

[1] © AQA 2007 Please refer to the current version of the specification on AQA's website at www.aqa.org.uk/over/extendedproject.php.

AQA assessment objectives

AQA Assessment Objectives	Marks awarded	Weighting
AO1 Manage • Identify the topic • Identify project aims and objectives • Produce a project plan • Complete the individual project, or task within a group project, applying organisational skills and strategies to meet stated objectives	Marks out of 10 within three mark bands	20%
How might I gain more marks here? You need to make it clear exactly what your area of study is. Writing a concise title, project aims and objectives, helps to focus what you are aiming to achieve, even if you refine your title at a later stage. Your project plan should be very detailed with clear evidence of how you will monitor progress against your project plan once this has been agreed.		
AO2 Use resources • Obtain and select information from a range of sources • Analyse data • Apply information relevantly • Demonstrate understanding of any appropriate links	Marks out of 10	20%
How might I gain more marks here? Make sure you select and evaluate a wide range of relevant sources, and reference these correctly. As you find relevant information and data, analyse it critically. For example, comment on its validity or how it relates to other research in this area. Relate the information and data to your project, by relating it to your own ideas and what you intend to do. AO2 also relates to using the appropriate skills and techniques for some projects.		

Chapter 2: Project management skills: researching the project

AQA Assessment Objectives	Marks awarded	Weighting
AO3 Develop and realise • Problem solving • Decision making • Creative thinking • To achieve planned outcomes	Marks out of 20	40%

How might I gain more marks here?

Make sure you follow your plan, taking appropriate decisions at each stage and collecting and analysing appropriate information and data.

Where your project plan has to change or you adapt your title or aims and objectives, make sure you provide clear reasons and explanations for these changes.

Draw your findings together, and communicate them fluently in an appropriate format.

Refer back to the aims and objectives of your project. Make sure you present information that communicates these logically and coherently.

| AO4 Review
• Evaluate own learning and performance
• Communication skills
• Convey and present evidenced outcomes and conclusions | Marks out of 10 | 20% |

How might I gain more marks here?

Provide a detailed and careful evaluation of the strengths and weaknesses of your completed project. Evaluate the process you carried out and your learning.

Make sure all your material is relevant, well structured and appropriately presented.

Your conclusions should be based on sound evidence and judgements.

Chapter 2: Project management skills: researching the project

Research methods

By the end of this section, you should be able to:
- identify and evaluate the most valuable resources for your project
- use the Internet effectively as a research tool
- establish codes of conduct if using people as subjects in your research
- recognise links in your research
- record and reference your resources to fulfil the assessment criteria

This section is about researching information and evaluating what you find. Before you start, think carefully about:
- what information you need for your project
- what *sort of* information
- how much information.

To answer this you need to think about how your findings will relate to the topic of your project, and the way you intend to structure your project report and/or the nature of your artefact.

Supporting your ideas with research

Think about the type of data and resources which would inform your thinking about your project. Try to develop your own ideas through an understanding of similar work already done. This does not mean your ideas will not be 'original'. It just means they are well-informed and evidence-based, and that your proposals or statements are backed up by evidence.

As an example, imagine a group of organisations competing to win a local council tender to design a skate park. No matter how imaginative, fun and attractive the designs, no-one will be impressed if the design is not backed up by research. In this case research might be around durability of materials and surfaces, national safety standards, recent developments in skate parks in this county and overseas, how people use skate parks, local needs and views of local residents.

Key questions for research

By now you will have a title for your project, which may or may not be a question. It is very important to give enough thought to your title, since your whole project depends on this.

To decide on what research is needed, you need to focus on the key questions about your project topic.

Chapter 2: Project management skills: researching the project

For instance, what questions might the designers have asked about skate parks? Examples might be: 'What are the most up-to-date surfaces being used in this country and abroad?' What UK safety standards do we need to adhere to?

ACTIVITY Focussing the questions for your research

Write down your project title, then write down three questions relevant to your research. These questions must be interesting enough to keep you motivated, and must be possible to answer within the time frame.

Now list possible sources of information relevant to each question, including any primary data you need to collect.

Explain how each information source will help you to answer your research questions.

Swap your questions and ideas for information sources with another student, and share some constructive criticism on each other's work.

Identifying likely resources

Sources of information to answer the question about UK safety standards might be government reports and other documents, survey data, academic articles and reports.

Other sources relevant to your project will depend on the topic, but might include publications such as reports, articles, books and newspapers, archives or geographical data. Secondary data products such as census data, longitudinal data sets or survey data might be used. In addition, you might collect your own data (primary data).

The sheer quantity and ease of access to information means that it is important to use effective searching strategies, then evaluate what you find. To support your research, you should look for professional and reliable information on the web, and also:

- in libraries (school, college, public, or those within local higher education institutions including universities)
- in archives of professional institutions
- amongst local professionals or employers: you or your centre may have already formed relationships with local organisations through work experience or voluntary work
- from charities and voluntary organisations.

The next section is about consulting a range of resources, including text books, the British Library, online journals, experts in the field, and surveys.

Books and journals

> ### ACTIVITY Books and journals
>
> 1. Visit your school or college library and locate any textbooks for your project area. Familiarise yourself with the books available, so you know where to look for information you might need in the future. Look up one key term relevant to your current study in the index of a selected book. Note the book title, author and page number, along with one new fact you have discovered on that page.
>
> 2. Locate one text book relevant to your project topic. Find the ISBN number on the back of this book. Find out what ISBN stands for, and how this number might be useful to you.
>
> 3. What type of publication has an ISSN (International Standard Serial Number)? Who issues ISSN numbers?
>
> 4. The British Library holds 14 million books, 920,000 journal and newspaper titles, 58 million patents, 3 million sound recordings, and a lot more – so this represents a vast potential resource for you. Go to the home page of the British Library. Click on Search Tips and Advanced Searching. Explore the links from this page.

Evaluating your resources

Because of the vast range of information available, it is important that you learn to evaluate the usefulness and reliability of sources. You might, for example, be able to rapidly identify a source as relatively unreliable. This helps you to use your research time more efficiently.

There is a range of criteria you might refer to when judging a source's reliability:

- **Reliability of the author** – Who is the author? What is the professional background of the author? What year was the information written? What is their occupation? Are they sponsored or supported by an organisation that has a vested interest?
- **Reliability of publisher** – What is the purpose of the resource? Is it to persuade or to inform? Who is the target audience?
- **Reliability of cited sources** – Can you trust the sources listed in the bibliography?
- **Reliability of information sources** – Is there a comprehensive peer review policy? Who are the experts quoted? Is the information complete and coherent? For example, do conclusions match the data that has been presented? Does the source present a balanced view or is there evidence of bias?

Chapter 2: Project management skills: researching the project

ACTIVITY Evaluating the quality of your resources

The following table summarises some criteria you could take into account when deciding whether or not the information you have researched is reliable. The table has statements missing in one or other of the two columns. Discuss the missing statements needed to complete the table.

Remember that you also need to assess whether the information is useful for your project, and whether it is at the right level for you.

About the author of the work

Likely to be reliable	Problematic
Recognised experts	
Work in a respected institution	Not connected with any recognised institution or organisation
No commercial or academic interest in the issues	

The publication

Likely to be reliable	Problematic
Reputable journal where articles are peer reviewed	
	Source which may have a strong commitment to one point of view or motive
Recent (is this always a good point?)	
	Produced in a country with political interference

Data

Likely to be reliable	Problematic
The difference between the intervention and the control group is large enough to be statistically significant	
	Small sample size
Unbiased sample: participants involved are placed in the intervention and control group randomly	
	Data collected from a group or situation which can't be generalised to the situation of interest to your project

Continued overleaf

Conclusions

Likely to be reliable	Problematic
Conclusions are backed up by the evidence	
There is an accepted mechanism to explain the conclusion.	Data might be explained in another way
	The conclusions are based only on a correlation

Checklist for evaluating your sources

Use the following checklist of questions for three resources that you have already collected.

1. How is the source relevant to your project? Is it at the right level?
2. What conclusions are suggested by the headline or introduction?
3. Who carried out any research that is being reported, and what is their reputation?
4. Who paid for the report or investigation?
5. Was any data collection or investigation carried out?
6. Where were the outcomes of research reported?
7. What do other experts in the field say about the research or report?
8. Would you be able to make a decision based on these resources? How might you get more information?

ACTIVITY Academic referees

1. *Nature* is a professional science journal, but the same principles apply in other subject areas.

   Look up the 'information for referees' web page on the *Nature* website (via 'Authors and referees' on the home page).

   A   Make a note of brief definitions for the following terms:
   - editorial board
   - peer–reviewer
   - independent reviewer

   B   Save the 'criteria for publication' for use in question 2 on the next page.

   C   What type of person is likely to be asked to carry out a peer-review in *Nature*?

Based on Learning Skills for Science and reproduced by permission of Gatsby Technical Education Projects.

Wikipedia

Wikipedia is a source of vast amounts of information, but is viewed with suspicion because of the way it is produced. Entries on the site can be written by anybody. Although there is some attempt to prevent false information being posted, there is no formal peer-review process. Many of the *Wikipedia* entries have extensive bibliographies (sometimes listed under 'References' or 'Notes'). This is an indication that many authors are using a range of information sources to back up what they write. Does this mean that it is a reliable source of information?

It is likely that you should only use Wikipedia as a source of links to useful material, not as a source in its own right. If you do use and reference material directly from Wikipedia, make sure you evaluate it in the same way as any other source.

ACTIVITY Wikipedia

1. Choose an article on *Wikipedia* with some relevance to your topic area, and make an assessment of how reliable you think it is. You should carefully read the text for evidence of bias and any gaps in the content that you think should be filled. You should also look at the sources which are referenced, to see if a broad range of sources have been considered by the author. Are the sources reliable in their own right?

2. Use the 'criteria for publication' from the *Nature* journal to decide if you would 'accept', 'ask for revisions' or 'reject outright' this article if you were on the editorial board of a journal like *Nature*. Make a note of your reasons.

Based on Learning Skills for Science and reproduced by permission of Gatsby Technical Education Projects.

Using the Internet effectively as a research tool

You are probably already familiar with using the Internet for researching information. You may be a regular user of Google, for example, to search on specific key terms. For the purposes of your Extended Project, it is wise to review your use of search engines to ensure you are searching effectively. Google, as a leading search engine, has a number of additional features:

- the 'Advanced Search' button
- Google Scholar
- Google Images
- Advanced Operators.

Try using other search engines. For example, WolframAlpha claims to compute responses to queries based on an accumulation of data collected from experts. Compare the responses you get to the same search on Google and another search engine.

Successful searching

One important rule for searching online is to know exactly what you want. The more precise your search terms, the more you will restrict results to what you need. Other tips:

- ✓ Aim for between two and six key words in any search. If you only put in one word, you'll end up with far too many results.
- ✓ Include the most important words first. Many search engines anticipate that the first word you type is the most important one to you.
- ✓ The main results appear in order, according to how often the sites are accessed by users. Remember that some results (such as those in the right hand column of a Google search) are sponsored results, paid for by commercial organisations.

Evaluating websites

You have access to a volume of information unimaginable 50 years ago. The Internet is the easiest source of a wide range of information, and an important research tool for your project. However there are no checks on its content. The user needs to be able to distinguish between good quality information and rubbish.

You need to:

- evaluate the quality of the information (see page 45)
- ensure that the information is at the right level for your needs.
- keep checking that it is directly relevant to your project: it is easy to become side-tracked by interesting but less relevant information.

The activity on the opposite page is based on Learning Skills for Science and reproduced by permission of Gatsby Technical Education Projects.

ACTIVITY Evaluating websites

1. Note down one key question related to your project topic. Find three websites which you believe are sources of information that will help you answer this question. Write down the URLs of these websites.

2. Evaluate the usefulness of these websites according to the criteria below, where 1 = most useful, 3 = least useful.

Criteria	Site A	Site B	Site C
Reliability of the author			
Reliability of the publisher			
Whether the information is subject to independent checks			
Presentation of the information (simple/sophisticated)			
Presence of distracting clutter/irrelevant information			
Usefulness of the links			
Date of last update			
Ease of access			
Level of difficulty (general use or specialised use)			
Responsibility for the website (Who sponsors it?) Hint: truncate each section of the URL back until you are able to find the sponsor.			
Relevance of information to your project.			
Sources referenced are just author's own/ sources include those from other experts.			
Website is personal/ commercial/ government/ organisation			
Lack of bias. Only one side of the argument presented/ hidden message present/ trying to persuade you or change your opinion/ some information is purposely omitted			
TOTAL			

3. This sort of grid is useful for evaluating websites. Are there any other criteria you think would be important when evaluating websites for your project?

Using people as subjects in your research

There is a variety of professional codes of practice which provide guidelines and ethical parameters for the behaviour of researchers. These guidelines may be particular to an area of work (such as the American Psychological Association's Ethics Code or the Market Research Society Code of Conduct), but they all aim to keep the individual being interviewed from harm and to protect their confidentiality.

ACTIVITY Codes of conduct

Research guidelines or codes of conduct in your topic area for using people as subjects for research.

Generally, you need to consider these three areas:

1 **Confidentiality** – protect the anonymity of your subjects in order to get good quality information and to prevent them from harm. Remember to treat people with sensitivity if asking questions of a personal or controversial nature.

2 Allow your subjects to give their **informed consent**. Tell them the purposes of your research, how the information they give you will be used, and how this will be published or made available to others. If you record an interview, tell them who will be listening to the recording. Your subjects should be given the opportunity to withdraw from the research, or to withhold the data relating to them at any point.

3 **Assess the risks** of conducting this sort of research. Your centre will have their own guidelines regarding contact with people from outside your institution, so make sure you follow these. Also bear in mind the reliability of the information you gather from interviews and questionnaires.

Conducting an effective interview

Before the interview

Write a letter to invite your subject to take part. Explain the purpose of your research, how their personal data will be protected and how it will be used. If you are writing on someone's recommendation, say so. Suggest how they can get back in touch with you to arrange a meeting or, if necessary, a telephone interview.

Draw up a list of questions to guide your interview or discussion: this might be a fixed set of questions that you will be asking all subjects. Alternatively, you may like to leave it a little more 'free' to allow for a discussion rather than an interview.

During the interview

Introduce yourself, explaining the purpose of your interview and how/why you think your subject can be of help. Let them know how long the interview will take. You may choose to make brief notes, or to make an audio recording of the interview so that you can listen more carefully later. It is polite to ask permission from your subject before making a recording.

Chapter 2: Project management skills: researching the project

After the interview

Review any notes you made during the interview to make sure you have included all the relevant detail. If you do this within a few hours of the interview, it will be fresh in your mind. Always write and thank your subject. Let them know how your project progresses and how much you value their contribution. When you've finished your project you could send them a copy of your report, or tell them what the outcome was if there was a product or artefact.

ACTIVITY Questioning style

1 When interviewing others, your technique will help you to collect the information you need without bias. Out of each pair of question phrases below, which one (A or B) would you select as providing a more effective questioning style? Why?

	A	B
1	Explain to me …	Have you got a system of …?
2	Do you believe …?	To what extent do you believe …?
3	Describe the circumstances in more detail.	Are you happy with the circumstances of …?
4	What do you mean?	What exactly do you mean by …?
5	Option 2 is better, don't you think?	Which do you think is the better option?

2 Discuss the effect of each of the following techniques in relation to effective interviewing:

- A Getting the subject's name wrong
- B Frowning at them
- C Looking at them when they are talking
- D Paraphrasing after they have spoken – 'So what you are saying is …?'
- E Interrupting
- F Listening for content and looking for visual clues.

Using questionnaires

What is a questionnaire?

A questionnaire is a set of questions which are phrased so that people can give the sort of information you are looking for. Everyone gets the same questions, so you can compare the answers. They tend to be used when you need responses from a large sample of a population.

Start by thinking about what information you need, and from whom. Make sure that you address the key research questions for your project. What sort of answers are you looking for, and what questions would elicit these? You won't get useful answers if your questions aren't right. Do not under-estimate the time it will take to get the questions right. Be prepared to have to change them several times.

A small pilot may be useful. Try out the questions on people who don't know anything about your project - this will tell you whether the questions are the right ones. Experts may give you the answers you are hoping for even though your question was wrong!

What should a questionnaire be like?

The first questions usually provide information about the participant (gender, age, profession, and so on), so you can link the data to the type of person. Put questions which need more thought at the end. The shorter your questionnaire, the more likely people are to fill it in for you. Just one side of A4 is ideal.

Yes/No answers and answers on a given scale of responses (e.g. 5 is high and 1 is low in a scale of how much you like a flavour of ice-cream) make questionnaires quicker to fill in. It is also easier to analyse this type of quantitative (numerical) data.

Make sure each question only asks for one piece of information. Make your questions clear and specific. ('Do you eat ice cream regularly?' may end up with lots of different interpretations of 'regularly'.)

If you want more subtle and individual responses, you may include open-ended free response questions (such as 'Give an example of an ice-cream that changed your life'). This type of qualitative (subjective or descriptive) data is harder to answer and harder to analyse, but may give more valuable information. You can limit the range of responses to qualitative questions by providing possible answers to choose from (multiple choice responses).

Using interviews

If you want answers to more probing or difficult questions, consider using face to face interviews. Interviewers can still use well-designed questions, but you can follow up unexpected or interesting responses. Interviewing is more time consuming than using a questionnaire, so this method may limit your sample size.

Recording your notes: when interviewing people you can use an MP3 player. Give each sound file a meaningful name and a date, so you can find it again.

Carrying out a survey or questionnaire

- Ask participants nicely and thank them afterwards – they are doing you a favour.
- Make sure they understand why you are collecting the data and what you will use it for (unless you have a special situation where this might affect their response). Get permission to use their data, and explain that it will not allow others to identify individual participants' responses if the data are sensitive. Allow participants to withdraw from the study at any point, or to withdraw permission to use their data.
- Make sure that your participants are representative of the population you want to study, and that your sample is not skewed in any way.

Chapter 2: Project management skills: researching the project

- Ensure that you have enough replies. It is likely that you need at least 30; you may have to hand out a lot more questionnaires to get 30.
- Online survey programmes such as Survey Monkey allow your participants to complete the survey online, and help to analyse the data for you.

Analysing and presenting your results

Make sure you allow enough time for sending out the questionnaire, getting responses back and analysing the responses.

How will you record your results? Do you need to summarise your data, for example by calculating mean values? What type of graph (line graph or bar chart) will be most suitable? If it is qualitative data, a graph may be less appropriate.

You could make a graph or chart in a spreadsheet program such as Excel. The same rules for what makes a good graph apply whether you produce it by hand or using software. Make sure you have a title and labels for any axes.

Researchers try to see patterns in their data. Longer answers to open-ended questions may need to be summarised in some way. You can make categories to allow responses to be grouped together, for example, ' people who describe an ice-cream when on holiday', 'people who make their own ice-cream', 'ice-cream linked to another pleasant experience'. This allows you to make semi-quantitative statements such as '45% of people link a particular ice-cream flavour with the people they were with when they first tasted that flavour'. Alternatively, you may just wish to comment on responses, without trying to group or link responses together, or to any pre-determined theory.

Once you have collected and analysed your data, decide what conclusions, if any, can be drawn from your data. How certain can you be of the conclusions (you may relate this for instance to the size of your sample, or the spread of your data)? Should you find out about statistical tests so you can comment more confidently on the certainty of your conclusions? How do your results relate to your research? How will you use the conclusions from your data to inform your project?

ACTIVITY Designing and refining survey questions

You wish to research the link between amount of time spent in a part-time job, and amount of time spent doing homework each week.

Write down one or more research questions. The questions should define the population you are interested in, and the range of activities included as 'part time work'. Design six questions, and try these out on a sample of 10 people.

Compare your questions and responses with other students in your group. Agree which questions informed the research questions most effectively. What were the characteristics of these questions?

Now redraft the questions in the light of your discussion, and try them out with a different set of students. How did the responses vary? What have you learned about the design of survey questions?

Reading strategies to help you gather relevant information quickly

Skim reading

If we read everything that comes our way in great detail, we would find that time would run out very quickly! We need to be selective and disciplined about the type of reading strategy we use. Skimming allows you to move quickly through the text, look out for key words, data and visuals, and gain an overall idea of the value of the text to your project.

Tips for skim reading:

- read the title, sub titles and any paragraph headings
- look at any visuals, photos and captions
- read the first and last line of every paragraph.

Scanning

Scan reading is about looking for specific information in a document. You would use scanning to find a telephone number in a telephone directory, for example. When scanning in a textbook, you might go straight to the index, then to the relevant page to find the information. Once you've found the information you put down the book and move on.

Detailed study reading

This is where you really need to concentrate to understand the content and meaning of the text. It is a reading strategy commonly used for coursework, project work and when you are preparing for an exam. You are likely to want to take notes.

What this means for my project

When you are taking notes, don't be tempted to copy out long sections. It is not a good use of your time, and will discourage you from using your own words when writing up your report. So, if you think a particular section is of value, write a summary of the main points. A visual representation, such as a diagram, flow chart or table may help. You should also make notes about the source, so you can reference it appropriately in your report and go back to it should you need to. If you want to copy down quotes, make sure you do it using a different colour. You must make it clear if you use direct quotes in your own writing, or this is plagiarism.

Link

For more information on plagiarism, see page 95.

Chapter 2: Project management skills: researching the project

ACTIVITY Understanding articles

1. The title has been removed from the following article, so you have lost this clue for what the article is about. First read just the first line of every paragraph in each article. Summarise the article for a partner, or make brief notes.

2. Now read the whole article and decide to what extent you understood the article if you only read the first lines of each paragraph.

Kirklees Council has been at the forefront in demonstrating the use of renewable energy technology. In order to help reduce carbon emissions it has pioneered the installation of photovoltaic cells and wind turbines to generate electricity on municipal buildings. Local woodlands are harvested to feed woodfuel boilers to reduce carbon emissions; at the same time, this improves woodland habitats for wildlife.

However, the emission savings made by using renewables are minor in the context of what we need to do. This is acknowledged in the national debate about how we move away from fossil fuels to alternative energy sources such as wind, wave and nuclear power. This debate ignores the gross inefficiency of British national housing stock.

A large proportion of houses are poorly insulated so that much of the energy used to heat them is wasted. Within Kirklees a decision has been taken to fund cavity wall and loft insulation for all homes within the district. The principle here is to apply technology appropriately and cost-effectively to deal with energy inefficiency and reduce the demand for energy. This is a much more sustainable approach. The council also aims to ensure that new houses and buildings are built to the highest standards of energy efficiency and have built in renewable energy installations, where possible, over and above that required by central government.

Based on Learning Skills for Science and reproduced by permission of Gatsby Technical Education Projects.

Recording your research

As you carry out your research, it is vital that you record details of all the sources you have used in your notes. This makes good academic practice for appropriately referencing sources. (If you are using Word, the 'insert references' facility is useful.) Use a grid similar to the one below to record details; this will form a bibliography for your project.

Type of resource: (Book/ Journal article / web page) ...

Title: ...

Year of publication: ...   Place it was published: ...

Author(s): ...

Are they experts in this field? What are their location, occupation, qualifications? ...

Page no. ...

For journal articles only: Name of Journal: ...

Date of publication: ...

For websites only: Date that you accessed the information: ...

Published 'Last updated' date: ...

Representing information in your own way

When making notes there are a number of techniques you can use which will:
- save you time
- allow you to reproduce ideas and information in your own words
- help you evaluate sources and select information from a variety of sources
- create links and connections between different strands of information and opinion.

ACTIVITY Ways of making notes

1. Think about the techniques you have used successfully in the past for making notes.
2. Discuss your ideas with a partner, if possible, to see if you can gain other suggestions from your peers.

Spidergrams
Look back at page 20 to review how you might use spidergrams to make notes.

Index cards
You can use index cards to summarise the information you collect, or use them to note key words and brief explanations.

Using tables

Organising information into a table is a good technique when you want to compare categories or record different views or opinions.

Non renewable energy sources	Advantages	Disadvantages
Coal	Large global reserves Widely available	Underground mining is a dangerous activity Public criticism/ environmental damage of modern opencast mines
Oil	Ready-made fuel	Supplies more limited than coal Gives off pollutants when burned

ACTIVITY Making notes

1 Choose one technique and take brief notes from the text below.

Behaviourists, such as Watson and Skinner, represented the extreme view of environmental determinism. According to them all behaviour is directly shaped and controlled through various types of learning and systems of rewards and punishments. Biologists, on the other hand, adopt the nature side of the debate, and believe that innate biological mechanisms and systems determine our psychological make-up.

Few psychologists now take either of these extreme positions and most would agree that our psychological abilities arise from an interaction between innate and environmental factors. Language ability is a good example to illustrate this interaction: there is now strong evidence that human language acquisition is an innate process. We are 'hard-wired' to speak a language and we possess an inbuilt mechanism that is programmed to recognise grammatical structure. However, the actual language that we speak, e.g. Chinese, English, French, etc., will depend on the language that we hear spoken around us as we develop. Similarly the range and richness of our vocabulary will largely depend on the models we are presented with. One interesting finding that clearly illustrates how innate and environmental factors affect one another comes from speech perception research in infants. Werker and Tees (1984) showed that infants up to the age of about six months can discriminate between a huge range of sounds found in world languages. However, this ability has disappeared by the time they are about nine months and they seem only to be able to discriminate sounds from the particular language spoken around them. In other words, an external influence, i.e. the language spoken around them, seems to have affected the plasticity of the brain and shaped it to adapt to specific environments.

From Chapter 5 'Perception' by Jane Wilson in the AQA Psychology A A2 Student book. Nelson Thornes 2009.

Chapter 2: Project management skills: researching the project

Using ICT to support your research

By the end of this section, you should be able to:

- use ICT responsibly
- understand how some tools of word processing and spreadsheets, and other ICT techniques can help you save time in your research

A computer can help you with your research and writing, but you should consider the health and safety aspects of working at a computer for long periods of time.

Take good care of yourself

It's unlikely, of course, that a computer itself will bring you any real harm, but the regular use of a computer has its hazards. To avoid excessive strain or fatigue, it is worth following these simple guidelines.

- Adopt a good posture

Make sure your chair is appropriately adjusted, so you adopt an optimum posture. See the diagram.

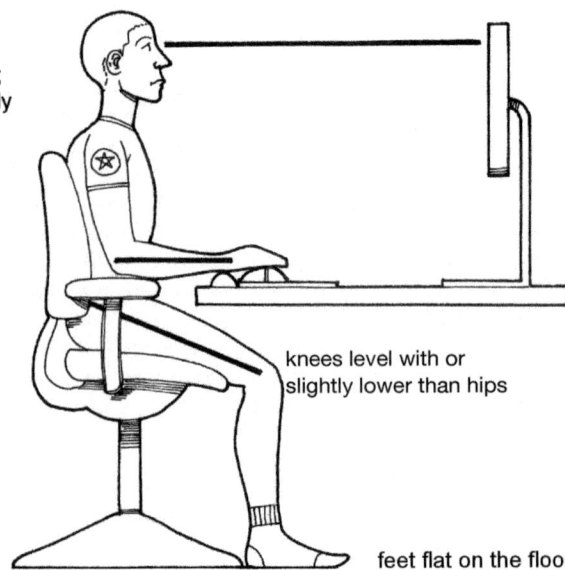

screen directly in front of you, not at an angle to your face;
screen at correct distance from you, so you don't have to strain to read text (usually about arm's length)

eyes level with top of your screen; screen tilted slightly away from you

lower back supported

knees level with or slightly lower than hips

feet flat on the floor

Taking good care of yourself

- Learn to touchtype

If you can type with two hands, you will put less strain on your hands and wrists. Learning to touchtype is even better, since it teaches you the correct positioning of your hands and wrists, and prevents strain from looking up and down between the keyboard and screen.

- Take short, frequent breaks

Taking short breaks will help to avoid RSI (repetitive strain injury), and also relieve your eyes from focusing at a single distance on the computer screen.

- Avoid glare

Adjust your screen so there is no glare caused by sunlight or lighting. Adjust the screen's brightness so that you are looking at it comfortably.

See the previous page too.

Storing and organising your data and files

Your computer hard drive or network area can hold data, information and media files safely until you are ready to use them, or to incorporate them into your report. Consider using an external storage device, like a USB flash drive or external hard drive, to back up your project work. Having a back up procedure is vital to protect all your hard work should anything happen to the computer. Never just use a flash drive – always have more than one copy. Store information in a form that is accessible on all the computers you use. Keep track of which is the most up-to-date version with dates and even a.m/p.m in the file names.

You may also need to consider the **confidential or anonymous nature** of the information in your project files. If you have agreed to retain the anonymity of certain subjects, make sure you are honouring this commitment. Keep external drives locked, or ensure that files are password protected.

With the amount of data generated, you will need a simple but effective system of organising and accessing information. Decide on your system for file organisation early on, before the quantity of files and information is difficult to manage. Remember to organise your Bookmarks or Favourites in your web browser too, so you can easily access useful websites.

Useful tools in word processing packages

As well as using a word processing package to write your report, it's worth exploring the other tools these packages can provide.

- **Word count.** There are guidelines to the number of words you should include in your final report. Word can help restrict you to these word limits. Remember that, depending on the version of Word or other word-processing package you have, it won't necessarily count every word.

- **Find and Replace.** If you decide to change your use of a word or phrase or to opt for an alternative spelling, you can use the Find and Replace facility.

- **Index**. Before structuring and writing your report, you could consider whether or not you intend to use an index. You can generate an index in Word (and insert citations and references). Deciding on which words and phrases to include in an index is an acquired skill in itself. It might be helpful, as a preliminary stage, to create a list of the topics and sub topics you think might appear in your index, then identify the words (entries). When you have identified the entries you want to include, highlight these ready to generate the index. Then follow the instructions in your word-processing software to create the index.
- **Formatting images**. Look for options on formatting images in your word-processor. You can usually fix the image in line with the text (to avoid them 'roaming' about as they often do).
- **Template**. Create a template that you can re-use to write letters inviting others to participate in your research. Although email is used for most communications in education and business, a letter of invitation will help your request stand out from a busy email inbox – and help you achieve your objectives.

What this means for my project

It's important in the early stages of doing your project to take a broad view of the different IT tools available to you so that you can make effective use of them. This will save time and stress in the longer term.

To save time…

- Keyboard shortcuts in word-processing programs help you to use the keyboard in a different way, or to reduce mouse use.

Risk assessment

By the end of this section, you should be able to:

- carry out a risk assessment relating to the potential risks involved in your project.

Students and researchers in higher education institutions often have to carry out risk assessments for their projects. Whilst this might seem natural for a science related project in a chemistry laboratory, it is actually widespread across all subject areas. Employers have a legal requirement to carry out risk assessments in the workplace in order to protect the health and safety of their employees.

What this means for my project

Even if you are developing a line of work which doesn't seem hazardous, for example, in the social sciences or related to MFL (modern foreign languages), it is still worth carrying out this exercise. If your project involves other people, or meeting external experts, for example, there may be health and safety aspects you need to consider. If your project involves a topic area new to you, you may need to consider unfamiliar skills or techniques.

There are six key steps you need to consider when carrying out a risk assessment for your project.

1. Look out for hazards and the potential for harm.
2. Be aware of who your project might affect and possibly harm.
3. Decide on the severity and likelihood of the risks, and what you could do to prevent them.
4. Review your risk assessment and revise it if necessary.
5. Having implemented your risk reductions, discuss your risk assessment with your Project Supervisor.
6. Remember to return to this plan after your mid-project review.

For more information on the health & safety issues in your particular subject discipline, talk to your Project Supervisor.

Chapter 2: Project management skills: researching the project

Drawing up a risk assessment grid

It is worth drawing up a grid to help organise your risk assessment report. The criteria in the grid will trigger your thoughts about different risks, including their severity and likelihood.

Risk Assessment grid							
Name:				**Project title:**			
	Severity of risk: what is the possible impact?			Likelihood of risk			Overall risk
Risk type	High	Medium	Low	High	Medium	Low	
Legal							
Financial							
Personal health & safety							
Health & safety of others							
Confidentiality of others							
Relying on resources							
Personal reputation							
Other:							
Detail the steps you will take to minimise the risks 1 2 3							

ACTIVITY Risk assessment

1. Carry out a risk assessment of your project.
2. Discuss your risk assessment with your Project Supervisor.

Chapter 2: Project management skills: researching the project

Skills to help your project run smoothly

By the end of this section, you should be able to:

- understand the value of applying critical thinking and analytical skills to your project research and development
- identify how decision making and problem solving skills can help you make good decisions more effectively
- apply creative thinking skills to your project to help you manage obstacles.

What do we mean by critical thinking?

Critical thinkers take nothing they read or see for granted. Useful by the time you are engaged in advanced level and undergraduate work, critical thinking skills require you to:

- refer to the model or criteria you are going to evaluate against (such as the status of the author of a journal article)
- carry out a careful and detailed evaluation of resources and materials used in your research, checking they are appropriate and up to date
- evaluate the evidence for any claims made by the author
- look for any potential bias
- weigh up all opinions and arguments so your discussion is supported through reasoning.

These are the main elements that make up critical thinking relating to research. These skills apply to a variety of subject areas and professions (imagine lawyers, engineers, or journalists without critical and analytical thinking).

Critical thinking skills are also valuable in daily life. Consider English Premier League Football where managers are easily dismissed as soon as their team fails to win a few games. One argument regularly put forward is that teams need a stable manager in order to succeed (teams like Manchester United and Arsenal are often quoted to 'substantiate' this). But should this logic necessarily be taken at face value? What this argument fails to acknowledge is that these managers are often stable because of success, not the other way around.

Seeing the whole picture

It's only when you see the whole picture, you know what is really going on.

Statistics may only tell part of the story

ACTIVITY Evaluating statistics

This table is from a Royal Academy of Engineering publication *The Cost of Generating Electricity*. Cost is an important factor when making decisions about energy policy. Consider the table below which shows the costs of electricity generation from different sources.

Source	Cost in p / kW hour
Gas-fired Combined Cycle Gas Turbine (CCGT)	2.2
Nuclear fission plant	2.3
Coal-fired pulverised-fuel (PF) steam plant	2.5
Coal-fired circulating fluidised bed (CFB) steam plant	2.6
Coal-fired integrated gasification combined cycle (IGCC)	3.2
Poultry litter-fired bubbling fluidised bed	6.8
Onshore wind farm	3.7
Offshore wind farm	5.5
Wave and marine technologies	6.6

1. Do these costs give us the full picture? Research the 'hidden' costs of nuclear power. In a search engine, type in 'cost of nuclear'.

2. Write down additional costs involved in producing electricity from nuclear fission.

3. What other 'costs' might be involved in producing electricity, other than economic costs?

Based on Learning Skills for Science and reproduced by permission of Gatsby Technical Education Projects.

Statistics: strengths and weaknesses

What do statistics tell you?
Scientists and social scientists are often interested in describing real-life phenomena, such as the economic market, sales, examination performance, or behaviour of students in local clubs. They do this by collecting data, then using these data to make conclusions.

It is important to have some knowledge and understanding of statistics if you wish to use data to support your own ideas. You also need this to be critically aware of others' use of statistics.

You have probably used graphs and bar charts to present data. Being able to describe data and use it to make inferences are useful additional skills.

Sampling and descriptive statistics
Researchers are often interested in findings that apply to whole populations. It is not normally possible to collect data from every individual in a population, so data is collected from a manageable sample of the population of interest.

'Populations' and 'samples': if you were interested in the behaviour of male sixth form students on seaside piers, your population is male sixth form students. You use the results from your sample to infer things about the whole population of male sixth form students. In order to do this, your sample size must be large enough to include most of the variation present within the population. The sample must be representative of the population, that is, not biased. If you only looked at students from sixth form colleges, your sample would be biased.

The mean of a set of values is often used to describe the data. Measures of how spread out the data are (such as standard deviation) are also important. Measures of the spread of the data are often shown as 'error bars' on graphs, and these should be taken into account when describing trends in data

Large sample size is important. Otherwise the mean of your sample may not represent the mean of the whole population. If you take a number of large, random samples from a population, you would not expect the mean to vary very much.

If you counted the number of sticks of rock bought by sixth form male students on seaside piers at two different seaside towns, you may find two different mean values. Depending on how different these means are, it may not be possible to tell whether this difference suggests these are two different populations (sixth form male students with good oral hygiene and sixth form male students with poor oral hygiene) or whether the difference you have observed is normal variation due to chance. You may need to perform a statistical test to determine whether this difference is statistically significant.

Correlation and causation

Correlation is an important idea, as when one variable (e.g. number of sticks of rock eaten) changes at the same time as another variable measured (e.g. number of dental caries), it is common for researchers to suggest a causative link (e.g. rock causes dental caries).

A positive correlation is where an increase in one variable leads to an increase in a second variable.

A negative correlation is where an increase in one variable leads to a decrease in a second variable.

ACTIVITY Correlation and cause

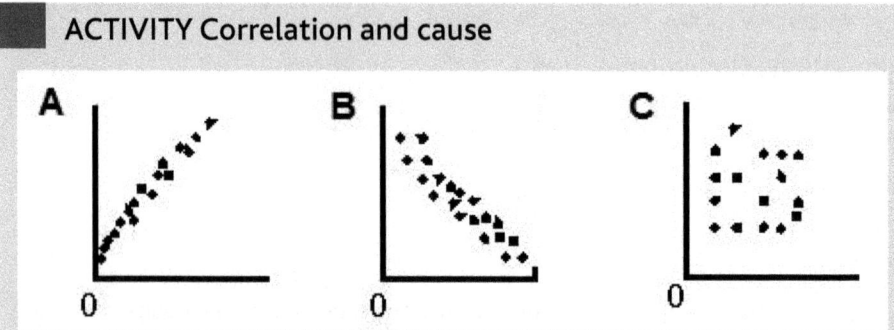

Look at the graphs A–C. Decide which shows

- positive correlation
- no correlation
- negative correlation.

Graphs and statistics can lead you to draw the wrong conclusions if you assume that correlation means causation. Comment on the following statements.

- People who eat Crunchy Oaties for breakfast are less likely to suffer from heart attacks.
- Higher global temperatures over time have led to greater numbers of pirates in the Southern oceans.

To prove causation, it is normally necessary to have an explanatory mechanism (such as how oats might reduce heart disease).

Correlation can be due to other factors affecting both variables. For example, global warning is increasing over time, and so is the amount of shipping in the southern oceans and the poverty divide in the southern hemisphere. Any of these, and many other variables, might be linked with the number of pirates.

Be critical of data

A customer satisfaction survey that asks people to rate a product 1–5 will show a different result depending on how the data is clumped. If a bar chart is drawn with only three groups (good satisfaction, medium satisfaction and low satisfaction) this could mask the fact that no-one has rated the product 5.

A claim that people young mothers are less likely to take exercise than other groups was based on a sample of young mothers in a mother and toddler group. Was this sample representative of all young mothers? Is any bias in the sampling likely to affect the results?

Here are some tips to help ensure that you can rely on the numbers.

1 Be clear about what you want to discover when you collect your data.
2 Make sure any assertions are backed up by evidence, and your report is not claiming causation when this is not proven.
3 Make sure that your samples are from your chosen population.
4 Ensure that your sample size is large enough . Your sample must also be random within your population, without bias to any particular group within it.
5 Some claims rely heavily on the mean of a data sample, but you should look at the spread of the data too.
6 Claims are more valid if the same study has been repeated with similar results.

What this means for my project

Remember that facts and figures may only tell half of the story. You will develop your critical thinking skills throughout your post-16 studies, and your EPQ will help. Like most skills, they improve with practice.

Assessment criteria for the EPQ require you to use critical thinking when evaluating resources and information as part of your project. In the same way, the approach you use to review others' writing, information, and evidence during your research should be applied to your own report writing. So, for example, when you quote a particular reference or source, you must be sure that it really does back up what you are saying.

Key terms

Critical thinking Also known as analytical thinking, it is a process used to analyse and evaluate information and arguments.

Decision making and problem solving skills

Poor decision making will hold up progress on your project, and use up precious time. Some people find decision making comes more naturally to them than others. However most students could focus on improving the quality of their decision making skills in order to make good judgements.

Decision making and problem solving are closely linked, since problem solving often needs you to evaluate and select from a range of alternative options. Problem solving can be applied to a variety of different situations; you can apply these skills to any task, activity, or decision related to your project – or events and issues in your personal life.

The process of decision making can usually be broken down into a number of straightforward steps.

1. Does a decision need to be made? What will be the impact if I don't make a decision?
2. Is the issue/task urgent or important, or possibly both?
3. What exactly is the main issue or cause of the problem? What type of problem is it? How have I solved similar problems in the past?
4. Draw up a list of all the possible options and solutions along with their pros and cons (advantages and disadvantages) (see section on 'generating ideas' on page 21).

'In any moment of decision, the best thing you can do is the right thing, the next best thing is the wrong thing, and the worst thing you can do is nothing.' (Attributed to Theodore Roosevelt)

> **Study tip**
>
> Don't forget to keep your Project Supervisor up to date with your progress. If you find yourself stuck and unable to progress effectively, do discuss this with your Supervisor. Your Supervisor can be a good source of advice and a sounding board, even if you feel you're making good progress.

ACTIVITY Decision making

1 Imagine you are having to make a tough decision, for example, whether to take a part time job, or buying a second hand car. Draw up a list of pros and cons for your decision.

Should I take a part time job whilst continuing with my studies?	
Pros (all those arguments for this decision; the advantages)	**Cons** (all those arguments against this decision; the disadvantages)
Total . . . pros	Total .... cons

Expanding the pros and cons decision making process

You can expand the pros and cons technique to weight your pros and cons. This allows you to take into account that not all disadvantages will carry the same weight or have the same impact. In the example above, you might think that having more money to spend on going out with friends is an advantage worth more than having money to save for a new laptop, for example. These weightings are entirely subjective – there is no right or wrong argument. The criteria will depend on your own personal set of preferences which may change over time, with your situation, or even with your mood.

You can use whatever scoring method you want to: you can score with 1-5 points, or an A, B, C scoring method or even award 10, 20 or 100 stars. It's entirely up to you.

The weightings may recommend you take a decision that you feel uncomfortable with. If so, you may need to look again at how you weighted different factors, or whether you missed out some significant arguments on either side.

With this sort of technique, you can add anything to either column that you think relates to your decision. This might also include emotional issues such as 'I'll feel more confident' or 'It will be a load off my mind'. At the same time, by listing and measuring options, it allows you to be more objective.

See the activity overleaf.

ACTIVITY Scoring pros and cons

1 Using the pros and cons you listed on the previous page, apply your own scoring method to weight the different elements.

Should I take a part time job whilst continuing with my studies?			
Pros (all those arguments for this decision; the advantages)	**Weighting score**	**Cons** (all those arguments against this decision; the disadvantages)	**Weighting score**
Total ... pros		Total .... cons	

2 How did the weighting scores affect your final decision?

SWOT analysis decision making process

SWOT analysis can be applied to help structure any decision making process. It forces you to consider issues that you may otherwise avoid in an instinctive, emotional response. It is regularly used in business to assess decisions such as 'Is this new business idea viable?' or 'Should we enter into this strategic partnership?'

A SWOT analysis would usually be presented in grid form with four squares, one for each of:

S: Strengths

W: Weaknesses (usually related to internal factors)

O: Opportunities

T: Threats (usually related to external factors; the outside world)

Strengths	Weaknesses
What are the advantages of this proposition? What are our strengths (such as people, assets, resources, IT, communications)?	What are the disadvantages? What are the gaps in our knowledge, capability, and so on? What would make us vulnerable?
Opportunities	**Threats**
What's going on in the world that would actually make this a positive outcome? What are the trends that we can capitalise on?	What are the external factors that would have a negative impact on us? What are the external factors that would create obstacles?

ACTIVITY SWOT analysis

1 Consider a decision you have to make about how to carry out part of your project.

2 Carry out a SWOT analysis to help you with your decision.

Creative thinking

Creative thinking uses less controlled and less predictable approaches to problem solving and decision making. The approaches should help to spark off new ideas, but can often involve some risk-taking. Creative thinking is where:

- you look for a combination of answers rather than one
- you allow yourself to play with ideas, to doodle, and to make any number of crazy suggestions which may or may not be 'right'
- you learn from what went well, but learn even more from the mistakes or extreme ideas you put forward.

Here are some ways of encouraging your creative thinking.

- Play with a puzzle or toy requiring you to use your hands: some people find that stimulating the tips of your fingers activates nerves in the brain, and this gets you thinking differently.
- Go for a walk along a different route. This allows your mind to work over an idea.
- Put on a type of music that you might not normally listen to.
- Do some things differently for a day, whether it's trying a new food or taking your bike instead of the bus to school or college.
- Try to come up with 15 different answers to the same question. Generate more answers by saying 'If I were in high spirits, my answer would be … '; 'If I were grumpy, my answer would be …'; and so on.

In fact, ideas can flow at any time – sometimes when you least expect them. Remember to note them down on your phone or in a notebook so that they don't get forgotten.

ACTIVITY Creative thinking

1 Select a situation from those listed below, and apply one of the techniques described above (or combine more than one), to arrive at a 'solution' or answer.

- **A** None of the subjects you invite to take part in your research accept, but time is running out.
- **B** Materials you'd planned to use prove difficult to get hold of within your deadline; your Supervisor suggests you research an alternative, but you are unsure.
- **C** You are doing your project in a group, but the other students are not contributing nearly as much as you feel they should.

What this means for my project

It is likely that at some point your project will hit an obstacle. This is not unusual. In fact, you need some obstacles to produce a good EPQ Production Log! You can apply some of the skills practised in this section to overcome any problems and decide on your next action. As part of your EPQ, you will need to describe how and why you arrived at each solution and describe any changes. Keep a record of:

- what the problem involved, and its potential impact on your project (in terms of time, money, the scope of your project, and so on)
- the options and solutions you considered, along with their advantages and disadvantages
- how you arrived at your solution
- the impact of your solution
- your evaluation of the situation. For example, how well did your solution work? What else would you have done differently?

Study tip

Getting along fine? Don't forget to keep your Supervisor up to date with what you are doing. They might have helpful advice or questions you've simply not thought of. They also need to have a good idea of what you are doing for your final assessment.

Your mid-project review

By the end of this section, you should be able to:

- understand the purpose of the mid-project review meeting, and how it helps you develop your project
- identify the most appropriate format for your project.

What your mid-project review is for

It is normal practice for your Project Supervisor to conduct a **mid-project review meeting** with each student involved in an Extended Project. Your Supervisor will decide with you the appropriate time to hold this discussion. This is likely to be when you have completed most of your research and preparatory work, and are ready to start writing your report or creating your artefact.

It is up to you to complete page 9 of the AQA Candidate Record Form, Production Log & Assessment Record. You may complete this during or after the meeting; you could make some notes on a draft copy of the form during the meeting and then write them up in full afterwards on the final form.

The purpose of the mid-project review meeting is to have a full discussion of what you have done so far, so that your Supervisor can:

- support and help you to decide on your final project evidence
- assess your progress so far in full.

What this meeting means in practice is that you will be able to:

- highlight any issues that might have arisen so far, and discuss any changes to your original project plan
- review your risk assessment and the precautions you are taking
- examine the best route forward, taking into account any problems and successes you've experienced so far.

 Remember the AQA EPQ Assessment Criteria

Remind yourself of the relevant AQA Assessment Objectives[1]. Use your mid-project review to check you are on track to achieve your best marks.

At this point, the relevant criteria are:

Assessment Objective[1]	Assessment Criteria
AO2 Use resources Obtain and select information from a variety of sources Apply information relevantly	'Evidence of detailed research involving the selection and evaluation of a wide range of relevant sources'
	In other words: Your research at this point may have thrown up huge amounts of data. You must now select the most appropriate information for your project. If necessary, refine the focus of your project, and redraft the title, in order to stick within the time limit and word length.
AO2 Use resources Obtain and select information from a variety of sources Analyse data Demonstrate understanding of appropriate links	'Critical analysis and application of the research, with clear links made to appropriate theories and concepts.'
	In other words: You need to make sure that you always reference the sources of your research and substantiate your arguments with appropriate evidence. Don't forget to keep a record of your research.
AO3 Develop and realise Problem solving Decision making Creative thinking	'There is clear evidence of changes to the initial project plan or title or aims and objectives, with clear and appropriate reasons for any changes'.
	In other words: Record the different techniques you used in order to overcome problems and arrive at decisions. Making mistakes or changing course can be positive. Just make sure you keep a record of the decision processes you used when making changes to your original plan.
AO4 Review To achieve planned outcomes	Remember you are limited by time and the number of words you can use in your final report/product.
	In other words: Review your progress against your time and word limits. Do you still think you can achieve your objectives within the time available? Is it likely your report will be within the word count guidelines? If your answer is 'no' to either of these you need to make changes so you can meet these criteria. Work out what gaps there are in your research and what still needs to be done.

---

[1] © AQA 2007 Please refer to the current version of the specification on AQA's website at www.aqa.org.uk/over/extendedproject.php.

Examples of students' work

Here are extracts from real examples of the mid-project review from previous students' AQA Candidate Record Form, Production Log & Assessment Record, reproduced by permission of AQA. You could discuss how well you think these students are doing.

Warning – these samples of work from pilot candidates may reflect earlier versions of the AQA specification and/or required documentation.

Project title:
A pastiche of a James Joyce short story based on a stylistic analysis of *Dubliners*

Outline the successes, failures, additions and/or changes you made as you followed your plan at start of project

When reading the novels I realised that … I was presented with three obvious options regarding the style I would adopt – I could imitate the 'stream of consciousness' in *Ulysses*, the development of language with age in *Portrait of the Artist*, or I could write a missing story from *Dubliners*. I chose to do the latter – and so began research into *Dubliners*. The state of Dublin is, obviously, a very important topic in Dubliners – as the stories focus on the lives of everyday, unremarkable people, living their lives in the city of Dublin. So I realised that the small amount of knowledge I had on Dublin needed to be expanded if I was going to write about it. …. I decided that rather than write the missing story in Dubliners I would update it, and write a story imitating Joyce's style, but about life in Bolton, in the 21st century. … Once I had decided this I researched Joyce's background and his attitude to issues with my own background and attitude in mind, trying to draw parallels between the state of society today and the state of society in Dublin when Joyce was writing. Looking at the technical side of his writing did not pose a problem as it could still be imitated – and although I have found that most themes can be translated to modern times there are some that are redundant – such as the union of Ireland with Britain – and some new issues that can be discussed.

Outline your planned steps to complete your project

I have read the introduction to *Dubliners*, and a critical work on Joyce … I have made notes on all I deemed relevant to my research. … I will read through my notes and make a general list of all techniques and issues which I will imitate in my writing, which I will refer to during my writing … After having come to a conclusion I will make a plan for my story – and begin to write it. Once my story is written I will then compare my own writing with the notes I have made during my research on Joyce's own writing and write an analysis accordingly.

Project title:
Given the rapid development and ever increasing funding for nanotechnology, and questions about its safe use, is it ethically right that it is so widely used by commerce and industry?

Outline the successes, failures, additions and/or changes you made as you followed your plan at the start of project

The main alteration that I have decided to make upon starting my project is to take out my section focused on the funding of research of nanotechnology at universities, as well as the funding of other scientific research. ... Specific information has been very difficult to come by, as I have tried looking in published documents and books, using the internet, and even a professor specialising in nanotechnology.... The professor seemed to be particularly reluctant to share information regarding the funding of the research carried out. ...

Your Supervisor's main comments and advice at this stage

I have been told by my supervisor that my essay is coming together well, but I must concentrate on citing my work properly. ... As a result of discussion with my Supervisor I have decided to bring another area into my dissertation. I would like to investigate the reasons that information about funding has been so difficult to come across ....

Changes, clarifications or additions you have made as a result of your discussion with your Supervisor at this stage

I have revised my methods of citing within my project, utilising the Harvard System ... The main problem with my work before this alteration was that I had consulted a wide range of sources in doing my research, and I had brought them all together to form my own opinions, which I then wrote in my essay, leading to a messy job in citing all these sources. I have now better arranged my ideas ...

Project title:
In areas of clinical practice, how successful have attempts been to combat the threat posed by viral Hepatitis B?

Your supervisor's main comments and advice at this stage

As we feared earlier I have got too much research and information, and my Supervisor has now advised me to stop any further research as I have too much of it and it will take a lot longer than we anticipated to edit my essay to fit the allowed word count.

Changes, clarifications or additions you have made as a result of your discussion with your Supervisor at this stage

I still want to include in my essay information that will allow the reader to fully understand my study, and this is impossible without including all the basic information. I understand the editing process will take a long time and that I will have to take large sections out of my current essay once it is finished ....

Project title:
How does Irish folk music reflect the social, political and economic history of Ireland? – a CD of 10 representative pieces

Outline the successes, failures, additions and/or changes you made as you followed your plan at the start of the project
Research was not as complete as I would have liked due to examinations and revision taking up time. However after research and discussion with musicians a tracklist has been produced. Some relevant materials have been found to use in the CD booklet.

Outline your planned steps to complete your project
Gather all relevant materials to be used in the CD booklet and start editing so it will fit. Produce the CD booklet using Microsoft Publisher and Photoshop on the PC. Go to Ireland to stay with my Dad, to record and produce a master copy of the CD.

Your Supervisor's main comments and advice at this stage
'Forget the research and continue with the main focus which is producing the CD.'

Planning your project product/artefact

The format of your end product will depend entirely on what is appropriate to the topic or task undertaken for your project. It will be useful to discuss this at your mid-project review. The format will be either:

- a written report of approximately 5000 words (which then becomes your 'product')

or

- a written report of at least 1000 words *plus* one or more of the following:
    - a journal
    - a piece of art
    - a live performance/CD/DVD/video/event/activities
    - photographs/exhibition
    - a product
    - a computer program
    - an artefact.

Your artefact could be almost anything as long as it's entirely appropriate and authentic to your topic and task. For example:

- If you are developing a marketing strategy for a new product, you could create a one page summary/handout and a presentation to pitch your idea to a company board.
- If you are writing a computer program, you could create a 'walkthrough' demo. of the product.
- You could write a travel journal to reflect a piece of geographical research.
- You could present a new design or product as if presenting it to the client who originally commissioned you.
- If you carried out a survey that showed a lack of understanding of a health issue, you could produce health promotion materials.
- You could research the needs of the over 60s, visiting a local city and creating a historical tour in line with their requirements.
- A local company may require the creation of a new customer database which you develop to reflect their needs.

The written report **accompanying** your artefact should provide an analysis of the content. It should define and reflect on the thought processes behind the artefact.

Study tip	Students achieving good results were those who had thought through the appropriate form of their final product and/or report with Supervisor guidance.

Chapter 2: Project management skills: researching the project

Checklist – are you ready for your mid-project review?

As part of the assessment evidence for your extended project, you are required to discuss your project with your Supervisor at a mid-project review meeting. This stage is critical in the journey of your EPQ, and if necessary, allows you to re-set your sights and establish the most appropriate format for your project evidence/product. Your Supervisor will be very willing to support you through this review process, but will be more able to help you effectively if you have prepared for the meeting.

Use this checklist to make sure you're appropriately prepared for meeting your Supervisor.[1]

	Your notes
I have evaluated the resources I found, to establish those most relevant to my project by …	
The way I identified the most reliable sources was …	
The range of resources that I have consulted appropriate to my project title include the following types of media …	
My preferred technique for note-taking to record my references is …	
My preferred technique for note-taking to record useful information and add my own ideas is …	
The best way I can make use of ICT to support my research is …	
According to my risk assessment, the overall risks in my project are … I have taken the following precautions …	
Examples of where I have applied the principles of critical thinking include …	
Where I have used techniques of decision making, problem solving and creative thinking I have recorded these in the following way: …	
The questions I want to ask my Supervisor at my mid-project review meeting are:	
What else do I need to do?	

---

[1] Filling in this chart is not an AQA requirement for your EPQ. However it may help you to prepare for a meeting with your Supervisor.

Chapter 2: Project management skills: researching the project

Project progress checkpoint

▶ 1 Project management skills: starting out

▼ 2 Project management skills: researching the project

Have you discussed your project at a mid-project review meeting?	Yes	No
Have you completed page 9 of your Candidate Record Form, Production Log & Assessment Record?	Yes	No
Have you considered and finalised the format for your end product/artefact?	Yes	No

▶ 3 Project management skills: producing the project product

▶ 4 Presenting your project

▶ 5 Finalising and submitting your project

⟩⟩⟩⟩⟩⟩⟩⟩ *Next steps*

The next stage of your Extended Project Qualification will be to create your project product/artefact and write your report. This will involve an evaluation and reflection on your work which will then lead to your final submission.

Project management skills: producing the project product

3

As a result of the discussion and advice gained in your mid-project review meeting, you should review your original plan. Make any necessary adjustments to your plan, keeping in mind the EPQ Assessment Criteria, and the need to work within the boundaries of time and word length.

This chapter focuses on the development of your project's product including your report writing skills. The skills developed here are likely to be useful to all students, whatever the subject area of your project.

This chapter will help you to:
- select the best presentation style for your report
- examine different styles of writing and develop your own report writing skills
- use the accepted protocols for referencing sources in your report
- apply planning and time management skills to your project product
- prepare for your end of project review meeting.

'Now where exactly did I find that quote?'

Report writing skills

By the end of this section, you should be able to:

- distinguish between the different models of report writing, and select the best structure for your report
- appreciate the needs of the audience you are writing for, and reflect on how this might influence the way you write your report
- acknowledge the different stages in the writing process and the benefits of re-writing your first draft
- define the overall structure for your report, and the elements the report is likely to include.

You will have to produce a report as part of your EPQ product. This is still so if you are developing an artefact or additional element as assessment evidence for your project. The report length varies according to whether it accompanies an artefact, or whether it stands alone as your assessment evidence.

Whichever type of report you produce, you will need to include the thinking or rationale for your work, based on the research you have done.

Selecting the presentation style of your report

Assessment Criteria for the EPQ require that you present your report appropriately. You are also judged on the quality of your communication skills. These are partly reflected in the presentation style that you adopt for your report. Once you have chosen the format for the report, it is important to stick to this and to the word limits specified. This reflects the requirements of universities and employers, where many publications, journals or companies ask that articles or reports are submitted in a particular format and length.

A written report

For the EPQ, a project which consists only of a written report should be approximately 5000 words. This might be an investigation, exploration of a hypothesis, extended essay or academic report. Where your report accompanies an artefact, your report will be shorter.

> **Study tip**
>
> It is important to keep within the word limits. Many students have felt frustrated when their reports have been heavily over length. This often relates to inappropriate planning of the report and a lack of clear focus when writing starts.

Chapter 3: Project management skills: producing the project product

You will have come across a range of reports during your education, and may have met many different styles of writing in your project research. Academic journals lay down their own requirements for style, length and format. You could look online, for example, at:

- Oxford Journals, published by Oxford University Press, and search for 'Instructions for Authors'
- Informa World (Routledge/Taylor & Francis), and search for 'Important Information for Journal Authors'

Here are some samples of different types of reports and writing styles.

From 'History Today', January 2009 – see their website.

A Woman at Waterloo

Andrew Roberts introduces the remarkable memoir of Magdalene De Lancey, wife of Wellington's chief of staff, who accompanied her husband on a campaign that climaxed in triumph and tragedy.

Reproduced by permission of History Today.

From Catalyst magazine – see the Catalyst website from SEP

'Tree power' by Janet Taylor

Humans have been using the warmth and light from wood fires for hundreds of thousands of years. Even now up to half the people in the world cook their food on open fires. Wood fuel is in the news again now because it is a renewable source of energy. At present almost all our energy in Britain comes from fossil fuels and in the long run these will run out. Burning fossil fuels also releases carbon dioxide and contributes to global climate change. We need to replace them with renewable and more sustainable sources of power.

Reproduced by permission of Gatsby Technical Education Projects

---

From The Times online (TLS), January 2009

Shakespeare and deep England: Jonathan Bate's eloquent evocation of the man from Warwickshire

John Guy writes: 'At last we have a new kind of biography of Shakespeare. Starting from Ben Jonson's description of Shakespeare as "Soul of the Age", and shunning "the deadening march of chronological sequence that is biography's besetting vice", Jonathan Bate selects only the material that, he believes, will help to reveal Shakespeare's cultural DNA.'

Reproduced by permission of The Times Literary Supplement, www.the-tls.co.uk

From Business Review, Philip Allen Updates

Extract from 'The credit crunch' by Ian Marcousé

The reward structure

Both in the USA and in Britain, investment banks encouraged staff to look for innovative ways to achieve profitable deals. Some were offered a bonus per deal; most received a bonus each year based on the profits their deals achieved. These bonuses might amount to £1 million or more per person. The individual could pocket that sum, knowing that even if the deal went sour a year later, the bonus could not be clawed back. It was a classic 'Heads I win, tails you lose' situation. What's more, the individual with the biggest bonus would probably also be identified as the best candidate for promotion, to encourage the others. Therefore, the logical approach for ambitious bank executives was to maximise their bonus-yielding 'profits'.

Reproduced by permission of Philip Allen Updates.

ACTIVITY Different writing styles

1. Look at the examples of articles above and on the previous page. Collect up a range of magazines and journals relevant to your EPQ topic area from your institution or local library or the Internet. Select a range of articles and reports. Consider their style by carrying out a review, using these questions to guide you.

    A   Is there an abstract? What role does it play?

    B   Is there an introduction? What is its length compared with the whole article or report?

    C   Does the report refer to a specific piece of research? What were the methods and materials used?

    D   How are any findings described?

    E   How does the discussion unfold? Is more than one point of view put forward?

    F   When and how are the conclusions explained?

    G   What illustrations or photos are included? What do the visuals add to the work?

2. A   Which style is most appropriate for the field of your own research?

    B   Create a template in Word or another word-processing package which reflects the format you feel is most appropriate to your subject area. Save the template so you can use or adapt it in future.

    C   Agree with your Supervisor to send your work to them electronically so they can check your template.

Using visuals in your report

Imagine a world with no visuals. How much time do we waste by using words instead of pictures? It is worth considering the role of illustrations, photos, and other images in communicating or reinforcing ideas in your report.

ACTIVITY Interpreting visuals

1. Work with a partner, and with some visuals related to ideas or processes relevant to your projects. Partner A describes a visual which Partner B has not seen. Partner A has two minutes to describe the ideas or processes being portrayed, rather than the visual itself. Meanwhile Partner B draws the picture from the description.

2. At the end of two minutes, Partner B shows their picture to Partner A. Discuss how difficult or easy it was to interpret what was being said. How similar/different are the drawings to the original? Was it difficult to communicate the ideas from the drawing? Partners A and B swap roles and repeat the process using another visual.

Activity based on Learning Skills for Science and reproduced by permission of Gatsby Technical Education Projects

Processing and representing data

Just as an image can enhance a piece of text and make it more accessible to a general audience, graphs can quickly summarise and present large amounts of data – making the data easier to understand.

ACTIVITY Processing and representing data

An environmental scientist is monitoring the air quality at different sites in Greater London. He has gathered data at six different stations. However, he has not presented his data very clearly, making it difficult to understand what it means.

1 Read what he wrote when comparing data from two sites, consisting of measurements taken during October 2008.

> Nitric oxide was measured at a roadside air quality monitoring station in Haringey between 1st and 12th October 2008. The measurements were in micro grams per cubic metre of air. The measurements on successive days between the 1st and 5th were relatively low, at 4, 8, 8, 6, 1. Suddenly, on the 6th, the reading shot up to 30, then swung back to 4 on 7th, back up to 40 and 53 on 8th and 9th then 8, 36 and on the last day, 35. On the same days, the site in Bloomsbury bore little relation to the Haringey measurements. For the same dates, the measurements were 8, 20, 41, 6, 20, 36, 8, 54, 80, 7, 9, 68.

2 Reorganise the data into a table, to make the comparison between the two sites as clear as possible. Now compare your table with one produced by someone else. Are they the same? Similar? Which is clearer and easier to understand? Why?

3 Choose the table you believe presents the information in the clearest form. Now, using the final data table, turn the data into a visual representation that shows the trends and patterns in the data. Are there any discrepancies between the two sets of data? If so, how can you highlight them? What annotations can you add to your piece of work to highlight the key information it contains?

4 Consider whether you should plot both data sets or average values (such as for a week at a time). Should you use a scatter graph, bar chart or line graphs, and is a trend line useful?

From Science in Society website, 2008

What this means for my project

Your research may have generated large sets of raw data. You should consider whether converting it into a data table will be helpful for highlighting trends and patterns. Once you have organised and processed your data to summarise the important features, select an appropriate visual presentation such as a chart or graph.

Consider any other elements you might like to include, and how these will enhance your report. Will you make use of quotes? Will you include text extracts, photographs or diagrams? How do academic journals or articles in your subject area treat these elements?

Chapter 3: Project management skills: producing the project product

ACTIVITY Journal article analysis

1 Read the extracts below (or longer articles), and use this grid to help you consider the features of the language used.

Features/language style	Comments
Is the 'passive' (the EPQ book was placed on the table) or 'active' (she put the EPQ book on the table) voice more likely to be used?	
Are the articles written in the first ('I did ...'), second ('you did ...') or third ('he/she/it did ...') person?	
In what circumstances is the past tense used?	
When might it be more appropriate to use the present tense?	
Do report writers use emotional language or objective, impersonal language?	
Do the writers make use of colloquial words or phrases?	

Article from *Gramophone*

Curtain rises on La Scala season amid dramas offstage

The annual December 7 opening night of the season at La Scala is traditionally a high-profile event but in recent years it has become just as well known for the dramas behind the scenes. Sure enough, as applause and occasional booing greeted the new production of Verdi's Don Carlo, ... tempers had barely cooled after a dispute over pay for musicians and staff.

Reproduced by permission of Gramophone

Article from *Catalyst*, April 2006

Venus Express by David Sang

The Venus Express spacecraft was launched at 3.30 in the morning on 9 November..... The trip to Venus lasts 153 days. For most of this time, the strongest force on the craft is the pull of the Sun's gravity. Once Venus Express is captured by Venus's own gravitational pull, the engineers at the control centre in Darmstadt, Germany, need 5 days to manoeuvre it into its operational orbit. There is no lander on this craft; it is planned to follow an extended elliptical path around the planet. This takes it first within 250 km of the planet's surface, and then far out, 66 000 km into space, before it plunges back inwards once more.

Reproduced by permission of Gatsby Technical Education Projects

> **Spas: How toxic is your 'natural' spa? by Erin Gill, *Daily Telegraph*, November 2008**
>
> Everyone loves being pampered but are the ingredients as pure as you think?
>
> Before you let your mind switch off, there is one niggling worry that might be worth investigating. What goes into all those body wraps, scrubs, lifts and refreshers? Is that facial made from 100 per cent fresh papaya or are there other less natural ingredients in it too? The short answer to that question is yes. In many cases the products used during spa treatments are not nearly as natural as all those references to algae and rose essence imply. Depending on what the products are designed to achieve, they may include detergents, synthetic fragrance, a range of preservatives ... the list goes on.
>
> © Daily Telegraph Media Group Limited 2008

> **Extract from *The Hub*, London College of Fashion, May 2008**
>
> **Future research**
>
> A key concept for Fashion Science is fashion as a vehicle to deliver greater functionality, satisfaction and delight to wearers across the broad spectrum of clothing and accessories for personal health and wellbeing, sportswear, casual clothing and high fashion. The challenge is to balance the drive for constant change and renewal, with its resulting obsolescence, against the industry's global economic importance in sustaining trade, employment and livelihoods. Some of the questions the Centre for Fashion Science will tackle include: Can consumers be persuaded to buy less but cleverer clothes and can consumption be reduced through intelligent application of science and technology to enhance fashion design and production?
>
> Reproduced by permission of Professor Sandy Black, London College of Fashion

Defining your audience

Academic writing is usually formal. However, it is important not to confuse formal language with complex, over-sophisticated or pompous writing. For the purposes of your Extended Project, you need to remember that you are writing for a general or non-specialist audience.

You might find this language level more in line with newspapers, magazines and some websites.

What this means for my project

> Identify the characteristics of your audience before you start writing. You need to imagine your reader as an educated non-specialist with little prior knowledge of the subject. Imagine they have a good general knowledge, so they can interpret challenging material if it is clearly expressed and appropriately communicated.

Chapter 3: Project management skills: producing the project product

Think about the language of your report

Classic features of academic writing

As well as bearing the audience in mind, academic writing has a number of typical features:

- It is formal rather than informal.
- It does not usually include colloquial words and phrases.
- The author writes in complete sentences.
- It is written objectively, so that the reader can understand what has been researched and studied rather than what the writer 'believes'.
- The writer is accountable for what they say, and can provide evidence or an argument for their ideas.
- It avoids sexist language and stereotypes, such as referring to a professor or judge automatically as 'he'.
- It is precise, using language efficiently and effectively (no waffle).

ACTIVITY Writing styles

1 Bearing in mind what you have learned from your analysis of the articles and from reading about the features of academic writing, decide which of the following versions of the phrases in the table would be more appropriate to your report. Both are acceptable – which do you prefer?

A	Several possibilities surfaced …		Several possibilities occurred to us	
B	This paper examines		We examined	
C	I hope		It is hoped	
D	It is suggested that …		This is…	
E	You can easily forget		It is easy to forget	
F	The data indicates		I saw from the data that ….	
G	This suggests		The evidence suggests	
H	Xxx asserts …		Xxx says ….	

2 The following words and phrases are considered to be informal and colloquial. Identify alternatives which would be more appropriate to your academic report.

Stuff, Lots of, Sort of, Go down (the shops), Lab, Nice, OK, Again and again

Manage the writing process

Plan your report or essay

Work out the overall structure in terms of the paragraphs or sections. Refer to your 'ideas shower' notes. Produce headings and sub headings for the entire report.

Make notes under each sub-heading to say what it will include, how it addresses the question or hypothesis in your project title, and how it links with the previous and following sections.

List the research findings and sources you will refer to under each sub-heading. Make a note of how these will relate to the project question or hypothesis.

As well as thinking about what to include, think about what you should be leaving out. Work out roughly how many words each section should have in order to achieve the overall word allowances for your report.

Also work out how much time you can afford to give to each section in order to keep to your schedule.

Write down all sorts of ideas for the different parts of your report

Write down the key ideas (on paper or on screen) that have emerged in your argument. Create sub-topics to each of these main ideas. This stage helps a great deal in organising your own thoughts. It should also give you confidence, as you set out exactly what you have achieved so far.

Draw up your conclusion first

This is an accepted part of academic writing and although it appears illogical, it's not. You have to know where you'll end up when you embark on a writing journey. It also helps create a more coherent report, with earlier sections leading logically to your ending.

Your conclusion should aim to summarise the 'answer' to your research and draw together the main points of your argument. It is not a place to introduce new ideas, but should bring an authoritative closure to your report.

Get writing – anything!

At this stage, it's important just to start writing. This will be your first draft, so don't worry too much about the accuracy or the flow of your sentences. It's the overall ideas you need to get on screen first.

Rigorously edit and cut

This is where you go over your first draft and improve it. This re-drafting will be far more effective if you've allowed a few days between writing and re-writing. Go back to the structure you drew up, and make sure your report is following this. Use powerful language not clichés; vary the phrases you use to convince your reader; and carefully review the language you use for arguing a point of view.

What do you think of the next paragraph? See the activity on page 94.

Keep sentences short because it is easy to lose track of an argument in long sentences which have lots of clauses and sub-clauses and which are divided up by a large number of commas, which are supposed to break up the sense of the sentence, but which actually add to the confusion, by introducing new ideas, cluttering your brain and preventing the main point of the argument from coming over. Read your writing aloud (preferably to someone else) to check sense and punctuation.

Beware the word processing spell-checker

This tool will only pick up typographical errors: it will alert you to a misspelling of 'their', but won't tell you if it should read 'there'.

Stick at it

There's no such thing as writers' block. You won't write your report all in one go; it will take time and a number of drafts. Discipline yourself to write at a certain time of day or week, and use this time effectively. The best sort of writing is rewriting.

Study tip	Readers often read the introduction and conclusion of an academic report or essay first. This gives a feel for the overall shape and key arguments. Put effort into these parts and don't accept your first draft.

Structuring your report

When planning your report, it's important to think of the overall basic structure and the different elements you need to include. Consider the role that each of these elements will play. See the activity overleaf.

Sections of your report

Beware! This table is jumbled. See the activity on the next page.

Section of the essay/report	What this means	Exemplar language
1 Abstract	**A** Summarises the research, 'answers' the main question, and draws together the main points of your argument.	i) On the other hand … In contrast …
2 Introduction	**B** This will highlight the breadth of your research, and make clear why these references are relevant to your own findings.	ii) According to the work of XX who asserted … (+ quote) XX argues that … (+ paraphrase)
3 Background research	**C** A stand-alone, succinct summary of the main report/essay, laying out the purpose of the research, the methodology used, the key findings, and the main conclusion. This section must grab and interest your reader.	iii) To conclude …
4 Conclusion	**D** Explains the issue or problem which triggered the research and allows the reader to know what to expect by summarising its outline and structure. Probably about 5% of the final word count in length.	iv) This warrants a fresh look at …

Section of the essay/report	What this means	Exemplar language
5 Discussion	**E** All the sources, printed and online, which you have consulted during your research, usually presented in alphabetical order. This allows the reader to go back to the original sources.	v) Richard T Shannon, 2008, Gladstone: God and Politics, UK: published by Hambledon Continuum.
6 References	**F** An analysis and evaluation of the findings, and an evaluation of your own learning.	vi) To illustrate this finding…
7 Evaluation of sources	**G** These include a note of the work of others that you have consulted during your research.	vii) This report will compare and contrast…
8 Bibliography	**H** Evidence of detailed research which involves the appropriate selection of sources which may be significant, unique, or provide an interesting perspective in the development of your findings.	viii) Xxx considered many perspectives… Xxx denies….

ACTIVITY Structuring and writing your report

1. Redraft the sentence on page 91 starting 'Keep sentences short'. The redrafted sentences should be easier to read and understand.

2. Consider how the different sections listed in the table on the previous page could be used in your project essay or report. Match up the terms used to describe the different sections with their appropriate explanation.

Now match up the exemplar language for each element. Add at least two other examples of phrases you might use in each of these sections.

Links

For more information on how to reference your sources and compile a bibliography, see pages 98–100.

What this means for my project

You need to select the most appropriate elements to include in your report, according to the style of your project and the subject matter. For most written research reports or investigations, the structure will be of standard academic format.

This means it has an abstract, an introduction, background research with all sources cited, a discussion of your findings, a conclusion and references (including an evaluation of your sources) with a bibliography.

For the purposes of the EPQ, your conclusion needs to include an evaluation of the outcomes of your project as well as an evaluation of your own performance of learning.

Study tip

The format of an academic abstract may be appropriate for you to include on page 11 of your Production Log. It should be between 50–150 words long.

Avoid plagiarism – get more marks for authenticity

By the end of this section, you should be able to:
- explain the meaning of the word 'plagiarism'
- identify pieces of writing that have been copied
- understand how you can avoid plagiarism in your own Extended Project.

What is plagiarism?

Plagiarism is passing off somebody else's work as your own. It can range from getting someone else to write your work to simply cutting and pasting extracts from the Internet. It can also describe an absence of referencing where you fail to acknowledge that an idea or argument comes from someone else's work.

At school or college you'd often describe this as 'cheating' or 'copying', and you know it's not right. **Copyright** law seeks to protect people's original work, making plagiarism illegal. Current UK law covers plays, musical recordings and scores, literature, audio recordings, artistic works, broadcasts and films, and published works. The law allows authors to control the way their work is used. This means that any original piece of work cannot be copied or adapted unless the copyright owner agrees to it.

Coursework is often run through plagiarism-detection software by teachers and awarding bodies. Even rearranging the words, if you express someone else's idea you still need to acknowledge that the idea is *theirs* not yours.

It's not difficult to imagine how and why people plagiarise. Reasons could include:
- laziness – not making an effort to come up with another way of writing a phrase
- finding it difficult not to repeat phrases that a professional writer has used very well
- accidental – cutting and pasting notes from an article online, or copying notes without referencing them, so you believe it is your own work when you come to look at it later
- memorising – learning words by rote can lead to 'regurgitating' words without meaning to
- 'no one will notice' – it is blatant copyright infringement if you decide to take credit for someone else's hard work.

> **Study tip**
>
> Detailed reading and note-taking can result in plagiarism. Try to remember the main points in what you read rather than write out the actual words. Sometimes putting the information in a diagram such as a flow chart can help. You will need to sign the Candidate Record Form (CRF) to confirm that the work you submit is your own. Discuss this with your Supervisor if you are at all unsure.

ACTIVITY Plagiarism?

1 This extract is taken from the *New Scientist* article 'Controversial forensic DNA test gets the green light' (published 11 April 2008). Below are three ways of rephrasing the material. Work out which one would not be guilty of plagiarism.

> Although Caddy's report backs the science behind the analysis, it criticises the lack of uniformity in the way that police forensics teams collect and interpret DNA evidence, and the lack of awareness that contamination with DNA could falsify matches.

A Even though Caddy's report backs the science behind the analysis, it doesn't back the lack of uniformity in the way that forensics teams collect and translate DNA evidence, and the fact they are not aware that contamination with DNA can falsify matches.

B Caddy has said that forensic teams do not all collect and interpret the evidence that they find. There is also the added problem of forensic teams not realising that contamination with other DNA can lead to the wrong conclusion.

C Caddy's report might have supported the analysis' science, but it criticises the lack of uniformity in the forensics team's collection and interpretation of DNA evidence, and that contamination with DNA could falsify matches.

2 Write down three ways in which you can avoid plagiarism in your own work. Consider how you take notes and make visuals from what you read. Which methods are less likely to result in the exact repetition of your sources?

What this means for my project

Your project requires you to develop your *own* ideas and arguments, and express them clearly. You need to discuss the work or opinions of others relevant to your project. You will certainly gain more marks if you can prove that you have 'obtained and selected information from a range of sources'. So, take great care to use quotes or speech marks to show that someone's words are not your own. If you want to include a longer extract from a book or article, for example a whole paragraph, the convention is to indent the writing rather than using quotation marks. Use appropriate conventions for referencing your sources (see pages 110–112).

Key terms

Plagiarism Copying someone else's work or recycling their ideas, and passing it off as your own either accidentally or through laziness.

Copyright Copyright usually belongs to the author of a piece of work (or sometimes the publisher) and prevents anyone else from reproducing their work.

Pages 95–96 are based on learning Skills for Science and used by permission of Gatsby Technical Education Projects

Referencing your sources

By the end of this section, you should be able to:
- understand the importance of referencing your sources
- appreciate there are accepted formats for referencing different types of sources
- understand how different referencing conventions are used in different subject areas.

Why do we need to reference sources?

There are a variety of accepted systems of referencing sources in academic work. These are usually based around broad subject disciplines, but they all have a common purpose. Referencing sources will help to:

- Provide your reader with details about where they can go for more information.
- Present your work with authority, following best academic practice to assure readers that it is based on verifiable published research.
- Offer your reader the reassurance that you have consulted a broad range of relevant published sources, topical or current in your field of research.
- Avoid plagiarism: by referencing other people's work you acknowledge that some ideas or phrases are not your own. (Even if you rework someone's words into your own, it is still a good academic discipline to acknowledge the source of the ideas.)
- Support the evidence of your report, substantiating your arguments.

Referencing resources

Many higher education institutions present their own guidelines for how they expect students to reference resources, such as the Harvard system of referencing. Professional societies or associations also have their own referencing conventions, as do the British Standards Institution. Follow the system used by academics writing in your subject area. You may have been taught some conventions which your current teachers expect you to use.

Some methods introduce more text than others; this might be important if you are close to your word limit.

> **Study tip**
>
> If you need any further help identifying the style of referencing you should use, discuss this with your Project Supervisor. Your Supervisor is there to support you.

How should you reference?

Remember there are two parts to referencing:

1. Identify another's work **in the main body of your text** to give a brief outline of the published work.
2. **Record your sources either in a bibliography or in a reference list** at the end of your report.

There are also different types of sources that you need to refer to – it's not just books and journals. These other formats may have their own styles of referencing which is important to follow.

ACTIVITY Sources to reference

1. Think of as many different types of source as you can – ones you might want to reference in your report.

Print	Electronic	Audio	Visual	Other
Published music	Emails	Recorded music	Film	

2. Consider websites.

   A What types of websites are likely to be most suitable for you to reference in your project?

   B Are any types of website less suitable for referencing in an academic context?

   (Think about the processes you apply when evaluating your sources.)

Top tips for accurate referencing

- When you do your research, note the style of referencing used in the books and journals you consult. This provides good guidance on referencing in your subject area.
- Keep a sheet of notes of *all* your sources from the day you start your research. This will help you to keep an accurate record, and it will also save you time should you need to go back to one of your sources.
- Once you've decided to follow a particular style of referencing, be consistent in how you apply it. It won't look good to mix and match the different conventions.

Key terms

Referencing Listing the full and original source so that readers might find it.

Citation When you quote or highlight a source in the main body of your text. If you cite a text, you point out to readers that the text or idea is not your own.

- Most of the information you require for referencing printed materials, particularly books, will be found on the title page or on the reverse of the title page.
- If you are in any doubt as to whether you should reference a source, it probably represents better practice to include it.

If you are using a direct quotation, make sure to reproduce it word for word.

Main referencing systems

Modern Language Association of America (MLA)

In literary subject areas, the MLA system of referencing is often adopted. It is an economical approach to referencing, providing the reader with the least they need to know. For books:

Highlight references in the main body of your text. Your text flags another person's ideas (+ original author's family name + page reference), for example: "One well-known researcher criticised Austen for her detailed portrayal (Harrison 221)".

Then list the full information in your bibliography/reference list.

Author's family name + given name + *Title* + place of publication + publisher + date of publication, for example: Harrison, James. *The World of Clementine Austen*. Cheltenham. Nelson Thornes Publishers. 2009.

To cite other sources, such as journals, online journals, personal communication, or newspaper articles, you will need to research precise guidelines from the MLA.

American Psychological Association/British Psychological Society (APA/BPS)

Very similar to the Harvard referencing system, these recommendations are relevant for psychology, health sciences, and nursing subject areas. For a full guide to the APA system, consult the *Publication Manual of the American Psychological Association*. For books:

Highlight references in the main body of your text.

An author plus date of publication system is used. For example:

"In a recent study, Brown (2006) found that there was …"

OR

"Beliefs in our own culture are often undermined by …" (Smith, 1967)

Then list the full information in your bibliography/reference list.

Author's family name + initial + *Title* + place of publication + publisher + date of publication. For example:

"Smith, T. *Psychology in Our Times*. Cheltenham. Nelson Thornes Publishers. 1967."

Chicago Manual of Style documentation system (CMS)

A scheme used for citing humanities/socials sciences subject areas.

For books:

Highlight references in the main body of your text.

The CMS referencing system follows similar rules to the APA and emphasises the author and date of publication when citing in the main body of text.

Then list the full information in your bibliography/reference list.

Although the first line of an entry is left-justified on your page, second and third lines are indented by five spaces. Arranged alphabetically, entries are:

Author's family name + (usually) initial + title/subtitle in initial capital only

ACTIVITY Referencing systems

 You will need to decide on the appropriate referencing system for your subject area. Research how this system advises you to cite the following types of documents:

Documentation	In-text citation style	Reference listing style
Books		
Journals		
Websites		
Newspaper articles		
Personal correspondence		

Remember that you will have to understand both stages of the process:

how to cite the work in the main body of your text

how to list the full information in your reference list/bibliography

---

Study tip

When referencing and quoting other works, try to avoid writing anything you don't understand. Don't be tempted to include something just 'because it sounds good'. You need to be in control of your own writing. This might mean leaving some ideas out as much as including others.

Key terms

Bibliography A listing of all the books, documents and online resources you consulted throughout your research.

Reference list A list at the end of your report which provides readers with more information on the sources cited in your work.

Producing an artefact for your project product

By the end of this section, you should be able to:

- select an appropriate artefect for your project
- reflect on why you have selected this artefect – and not any other
- apply the principles of good planning and time management practice to the development of your project product.

Selecting an appropriate product for your project

All students engaged on an Extended Project have to produce a report (some longer than others – see page 12). Some students will also develop an artefact as assessment evidence.

This may include:

- an artefact, model or construction
- a CD/video/DVD of an artistic or musical performance or activity
- an audio recording or multimedia presentation
- a journal of activities or events
- a slide or PowerPoint presentation
- a portfolio or exhibition of photographs to record a project
- a computer program
- a musical score.

It may be that the selection of your artefact will arise naturally from the topic and the original project title. For example:

- From an investigation into a particular film genre, you might compile a series of film clips on CD or create your own extract in the same style.
- You may be responding to a brief to update a business software package and produce your solution as a computer program.

If you produce an artefact of this sort, you will also need to present a written report of more than 1000 words.

Chapter 3: Project management skills: producing the project product

AQA EPQ Assessment Criteria[1]

Remind yourself of the AQA Assessment Objectives, and check you are on track to achieve the best marks. The relevant criteria are as shown in the table below. Use the **AQA Project Production Log & Assessment Record** (page 11) to record this process.

What if my project doesn't immediately imply an artefact?

For some projects, an artefact might be inappropriate or unnecessary. The project report could then be the only project 'product'. In this case, your report should be approximately 5000 words long.

Assessment Objective		Assessment Criteria
AO3 Develop and realise	Problem solving Decision making Creative thinking	'Candidates communicate their findings fluently in an appropriate format, synthesizing information from a variety of sources and present them within a logical and coherent structure which addresses closely the nature of the task.'
		In other words: Record the different processes and techniques you used in order to overcome problems and arrive at a decision.
AO3 Develop and realise	To achieve planned outcomes	Remember you are limited by time to create your final report/product.
		In other words: Review your progress against your time and word limits. Do you still think you can achieve your objectives within the time available?
AO4 Review	Convey and present evidenced outcomes and conclusions	'Material is consistently relevant, well-structured and appropriately presented.'
		In other words: You need to reassure yourself that you have evaluated all available resources and carried out a detailed analysis of the needs of your project. Your project should reflect the required outcomes.
AO4 Review	Communication skills Convey and present evidenced outcomes and conclusions	'Candidates communicate their findings and conclusions which are based on some evidence and judgement.'
		In other words: You need to provide evidence that you have applied the same skills of resource evaluation and decision making to your project product as you did for your project report.

---

[1] © AQA 2007 Please refer to the current version of the specification on AQA's website at www.aqa.org.uk/over/extendedproject.php.

Checklist – are you ready for your end-of-project review?

As part of the assessment evidence for your Extended Project, you are required to discuss your project with your Supervisor at an end-of-project review meeting. This stage is important in the journey of your EPQ. It allows you to review your work, highlight successes and failures, and help you to make any changes or additions to get better marks. Your Supervisor will be very willing to discuss this review process, and to support you in completing page 10 of your AQA Production Log & Assessment Record.

Use this checklist to make sure you're appropriately prepared. [1]

The best style of presentation for my report is …	
The different features I will use in my report are …	
The audience for my report can be described as …	
The best way to communicate my findings and ideas to my audience is …	
I will make sure I use the most appropriate language and terminology by …	
I will avoid plagiarism by …	
The planned sections of my report are ………	
The planned word count for each section is ………	
I have backed up my findings by ………	
The most appropriate referencing system for my report is …………	
The questions I want to ask my Supervisor at my end-of-project review meeting are:	
What else do I need to do? By when? (give date)	

---

[1] Filling in this chart is not an AQA requirement for your EPQ. However it may help you to prepare for a meeting with your Supervisor.

Chapter 3: Project management skills: producing the project product

Producing an artefact for your project product

▶ 1 Project management skills: starting out

▶ 2 Project management skills: researching the project

▼ 3 Project management skills: producing the project product

Have you discussed your project at an end-of-project review meeting?	Yes	No
Have you completed page 10 of your AQA Project Production Log & Assessment Record?	Yes	No
Have you considered and finalised the format for your report and end product/artefact?	Yes	No

▶ 4 Presenting your project

▶ 5 Finalising and submitting your project

⟩⟩⟩⟩⟩⟩⟩⟩ *Next steps*

The next stage of your Extended Project Qualification will be to plan and deliver the presentation of your project. This would usually take the form of a verbal presentation, and it may involve the use of slides, PowerPoint, or short excerpts of video material. If you are working as part of a group, it may take the form of a group presentation. You will also need to answer any questions from your Supervisor.

Presenting your project

4

It takes a great deal of courage to present your own work to an audience. Whatever form you decide on for your project presentation, good preparation will help you to relax and enjoy the experience. You should aim to present your work and the evidence of what you've learned in the most effective and interesting way for your audience.

This chapter will help you to:

- identify the best style of presentation for your project
- explore the structure of your presentation
- understand the pros and cons of presentation software
- communicate your message clearly and appropriately for your audience
- prepare and deliver a short verbal presentation
- overcome nerves and respond confidently to questions during your presentation.

Some people are natural communicators, but most people can improve with practice.

Chapter 4: Presenting your project

Different presentation styles: what should your presentation consist of?

Learning objectives

By the end of this section, you should be able to:

- identify good and bad practice in the delivery of a presentation
- explore which form your own presentation might take
- understand the objectives of your presentation and decide what it is best to include – and leave out of – your presentation.

Different styles of presentation

Your presentation can take a variety of forms[1]:

- verbal presentation to a small or large audience
- viva-style presentation where you present in a face-to-face situation to your Supervisor
- exhibition which might involve flipcharts, posters, OHP transparencies, presentation software, or video or audio extracts
- group presentation (as long as each individual's contribution is identifiable).

To help you decide on the form your presentation will take, it's worth considering good and bad practice and thinking about your own strengths and weaknesses. Would a short verbal presentation best represent you and your project work, for example?

---

[1] © AQA 2007 Please refer to the current version of the specification on AQA's website at www.aqa.org.uk/over/extendedproject.php.

ACTIVITY Thinking about presentations

1 Think about some presentations you have been a part of the audience for. Note down:

- characteristics of talks you have enjoyed (good practice)
- characteristics of talks that have bored you (bad practice).

2 Think about your own strengths and weaknesses. Give yourself marks out of ten for each of these statements, depending on how closely you believe they match you.

	1-6 marks	7 marks or more
I rarely suffer nerves when talking about something that really interests me		
I love getting up in front of an audience and am used to taking the stage		
I enjoy being challenged by unexpected questions		
I'm never fazed by an audience, whether of 2 or 102!		
If I prepare well and schedule my timings carefully, I usually do well		

What should your presentation consist of?

You need to balance what you want to say with what your audience wants to hear. People like to hear an enthusiast talk about what interests them, but be aware of what will interest your particular audience. Your presentation has to suit a **non-specialist** audience. Avoid jargon unless you understand and can fully explain this level of technical vocabulary.

Think about the structure of your presentation

Structure your presentation so that it has three main sections:

1. **Introduction**: or 'Tell your audience what you are going to tell them.' Let them know how long it will take, say briefly what you will talk about in each section of the presentation, and say why you are the best person to present this topic.
2. **The main section**: 'Tell them.' This should cover both the content and process of your project.
3. **Conclusion**: 'Tell them what you've told them.' Sum up your key messages.

Think about the venue

Where you deliver your presentation will affect the content and form it should take. Think about:

- What resources are available? Is there a projector or video screen you can use, for example?
- Are there any constraints in terms of space, lighting, audience size, and so on?

What this means for my project

Discuss the best style of presentation for your project with your Supervisor. Talk about what resources you need to prepare to match the content of your project, what you want to say, and the resources you have available. You also need to be ready to answer questions.

During the presentation you will be assessed by your Supervisor. Your Supervisor will ask questions that:

- explore your understanding of the project's material – its **content**
- explore the **process** of your project, and ask why you made particular choices during your research and production work.

Study tip

For assessment purposes, you need to demonstrate what you have learned. Just using long words will not convince your audience that you know what you are talking about. It is better to use everyday language and avoid jargon. Better still, use the necessary technical language, carefully explaining what it means. You have to be a real expert to be able to explain complex ideas at a simple level. You could use metaphors or carefully chosen diagrams to 'teach' your audience and demonstrate your expertise. ('Breaking the ice' is an example of a metaphor.)

Presentation skills

By the end of this section, you should be able to:

- identify the pros and cons of using presentation software
- make use of some techniques for getting your message across effectively
- manage your nerves during the presentation
- rehearse your presentation, including preparing for questions.

Using presentation software

Probably the worst way to start with planning your presentation is by starting to put together a set of electronic slides. Your presentation software is produced for the benefit of your audience, not for you, the presenter. It is not a presentation in itself but a support or visual aid to enhance your presentation.

It's probably best to plan the structure and content of your presentation before you put the slides together. The slides then form a back up or reinforcement of your message rather than driving what you say.

ACTIVITY Using presentation software: pros and cons

1. Think about the pros and cons of using a software presentation package. Consider:

   A the presenter's needs

   B the audience's experience

   C how the presentation software might affect the delivery of the message

	Pros	Cons
a)		
b)		
c)		

Golden rules for presentation slides to wow your audience

- Keep flying objects, sound effects, choice of colours, and animations to a minimum: avoid visual chaos.
- Create the right number of slides for the time you have available (roughly one per minute).
- Carefully edit and proof read your slides (before your audience does).
- Use the same font size throughout. Check you can read it at the distance of your audience. Keep text to a minimum. The words are just a short prompt for you.
- Only use capital letters for emphasis or impact: they imply that you're SHOUTING at your audience.
- Provide hand-outs for sections of text your audience needs to read, or for complex diagrams and data which will not come across effectively on slides.

ACTIVITY Props and visual aids

1. What other items might you use as a prop or visual aid to emphasise a point? Think of examples of each of:
    - something for your audience to taste
    - something for your audience to listen to
    - something for your audience to touch
    - something for your audience to try out
    - a moving image or video clip for your audience to watch.

ACTIVITY Assessing visual aids

1. Think about these questions in relation to your own slide presentation and visual aids.
    - A Does each slide or visual aid add a useful and important message?
    - B Will everyone, including those at the back of the room, be able to read all the slides and see the visual aids?
    - C Are there any slides where a picture, diagram or photo enhances your message better than text?
    - D Is each slide clear and simple: no more than six lines of text?
2. Switch off your computer and sketch out one slide for each main section of your presentation. These are probably the only slides that you'll need. Look again and reassure yourself that each slide needs to be there.

Chapter 4: Presenting your project

■ Communicating clearly

Clear communication is made up of several factors. You engage your audience through your personality and though your interaction with them, as well as through what you have to say.

No doubt, nerves are going to play their part. However, always remember that the audience or panel for your EPQ presentation will be sympathetic and keen that you do well. They're on your side!

Using body language effectively

When you are talking to someone, research suggests that the meaning of what you are saying is conveyed via the words you use, the tone of your voice and your body language – in the following proportions:

55% body language

38% the tone of your voice

7% the words you use.

Surprising, isn't it? But we all know that feelings show on people's faces even before we hear what they are saying.

This doesn't necessarily mean that you should fake or develop your body language, but simply to be more aware of it and use it to your advantage. Positive posture can add impact to what you are saying.

A friend could film you on their phone so you can watch yourself critically!

> **Study tip**
>
> The old cliché that a picture tells a thousand words may be true. Sometimes it's more effective to think in terms of what a slide shows rather than what it says. Remember that the media or format of your presentation must be entirely in line with the type of project.

> **Key term**
>
> **Body language** Our subconscious mannerisms, facial expressions, hand gestures, eye contact, and all those aspects of non-verbal communication which enhance (or possibly detract from) a message.

ACTIVITY Body language

Consider these examples of body language and behaviour. Discuss which you think would be most effective in your own presentation:

1A   You enter a room to listen to a presentation. The speaker has arrived, and is standing ready at the front of the room.

or

1B   Sitting in the audience you are waiting for the speaker. He arrives, rushing into the room, looking for a socket to plug his laptop into.

2A   A presenter stands with a folder clasped to their chest while speaking.

or

2B   A presenter stands facing the audience with their feet slightly apart, arms moving naturally.

3A   A presenter gesticulates with their hands and arms in a way which emphasises their enthusiasm.

or

3B   A presenter repeatedly fiddles with their hair and clothing.

4A   A presenter looks down at the floor while speaking.

or

4B   A presenter maintains eye contact with different members of the audience.

Positive posture might include:
- ✓ Facing the audience when you are describing the content of a slide, rather than turning to face the slide
- ✓ Standing with shoulders back and head up rather than hunching over your notes
- ✓ Thinking 'tall' (imagine someone is pulling a thread attached to the top of your head) – this automatically helps you adopt a more confident posture
- ✓ Arriving before your audience, so that you 'own' the space
- ✓ Standing in front of a desk or table to make you appear more confident. Behind it, you'll look more nervous and defensive.

Dealing with nerves

How do you feel about presenting your project? Nervous? Research has shown that the number one fear for most adults is public speaking. Even the most experienced presenters have to focus on overcoming their nerves before getting up in front of an audience or panel.

More often than not, we appear more nervous to ourselves than to our audience. Presentation nerves are usually driven by a fear of what might go wrong. So, once you get started, if you have planned well and practised your presentation, you know your equipment is working and your audience look interested, the nerves often subside.

ACTIVITY Dealing with nerves

1. When was the last time you felt nervous?
   - How does it affect how you speak? Do you speak more quickly or more slowly?
   - Does your mouth run away with you so that you speak before you think?
   - Do you giggle or appear more sullen?
   - Do you pretend you don't suffer from nerves at all, and come across as 'not really you' or maybe a bit arrogant?
2. Have you tried out any techniques to manage these nerves? Ask your friends or teachers how they manage nerves.

Familiarity brings confidence

Once you've decided on what you're going to say, and your slides and visual aids are prepared, you need to rehearse your presentation. This will help you to feel comfortable with your subject and with your timings.

A rehearsal stage will help you to:

- **Talk through your presentation** rather than read your notes.
  - ✓ Start by typing your presentation as if you were going to read it.
  - ✓ Use a large font and double line spacing to keep it clear.
  - ✓ Read it through a few times silently.
  - ✓ Then read it aloud.
  - ✓ Read it aloud while standing up – possibly in front of a mirror.
  - ✓ Read through it and practise the sort of arm movements or facial expressions you would normally use.

This rehearsal process will help you remember much of what you need to say and make it sound entirely natural. Familiarity brings confidence. Your notes will then be a useful prompt only if you need them.

- Familiarise yourself with the venue and with any equipment such as a data projector, to help you feel more 'at home'.
- Time your presentation and keep to schedule. When you are planning your presentation, allocate a number of minutes to each section. When practising, check your timings against a watch. During your presentation, place a clock or watch where you can see it without looking down at your wrist.
- Discuss your presentation with your Supervisor. They will be able to advise you on how to prepare.

Memory tips

If you have memorised your presentation, this will help you to feel more confident and relaxed. There is no need to memorise it word-for-word, but it is important to have a way of remembering the sequence of ideas you will present.

Use prompt cards rather than full notes, so the key themes and ideas are summarised and you can remind yourself at a glance.

Use a memory strategy such as mnemonics or 'use of *loci* (places)' to help order your ideas. Use an online search engine to find out more about these.

ACTIVITY Researching memory techniques

Research a memory technique which is useful for remembering lists of items or ideas. Explain this technique to two other students, and listen to the ideas they have researched.

Preparing for questions

Your Supervisor will be required to ask questions about your presentation. They will be looking to:

- explore your understanding of the topic
- gauge the choices you made in your research and the production of your project.

Examples of the type of question you may be asked

- Tell me about how you arrived at this topic choice.
- Why is your topic important?
- Describe one of the problems you faced, and how you arrived at a solution.
- Outline any additions or changes you made as a result of one of your review meetings.
- If you had to advise someone on doing a project like yours, what one piece of advice would you give?
- Could you explain exactly what you mean by 'xxx'?

What should you do if you get a difficult question? Allow yourself space to think about your answer rather than launching straight in. Don't try and bluff an answer. If you really don't know, say so, and suggest ways that you could find out the answer.

Chapter 4: Presenting your project

Checklist – are you ready for your presentation and question and answer session?

As part of the assessment evidence for your Extended Project, you are required to present your project work to your Supervisor (and possibly others). You need to prepare well and to bear in mind who your presentation is for. You want to present your work in the best light, so that you can demonstrate exactly what you've learned, and provide evidence of the skills you've developed.

You may also seek advice from your Supervisor in advance of the presentation itself. This, in turn, will support you in completing page 12 of your AQA Production Log & Assessment Record.

Use this checklist to make sure you're appropriately prepared.[1]

	Comments on your next steps	
I have discussed ideas for my presentation with my Supervisor, and the form it will take is ...		
The points of good and bad practice I have considered are ...	Good practice	Bad practice
PowerPoint will/ will not be an appropriate software package for me to use because ...		
The skills I will draw on to create my slide presentation are ...		
The questions I will be prepared to answer during the presentation include ...		

Chapter 4: Presenting your project

	Comments on your next steps	
The main points about the content and process of my project which I will cover in my presentation are ...	Content	Process
I've rehearsed my presentation either in front of the mirror or in front of an audience, and my reflections on the practice presentation are ...	Good points	Points I could improve on
I've timed my presentation and it takes ...	.... minutes	
The features of my body language that I could improve on are ...		
The particular needs, areas of interest and level of prior knowledge of my audience are ...		
I've had a look at the venue for my presentation, and the points to note are ...		
What else do I need to do?		

---

[1] Filling in this chart is not an AQA requirement for your EPQ. However it may help you to prepare for a meeting with your Supervisor.

Chapter 4: Presenting your project

Project progress checkpoint

▶ 1 Project management skills: starting out

▶ 2 Project management skills: researching the project

▶ 3 Project management skills: producing the project product

▼ 4 Presenting your project

Have you discussed your presentation with your Supervisor?	Yes	No
Have you given your presentation?	Yes	No
Have you completed page 12 of your AQA Project Production Log & Assessment Record?	Yes	No

▶ 5 Finalising and submitting your project

 **Next steps**

The next stage of your Extended Project Qualification is to finalise your project. This will involve an evaluation of your work which will then lead to your final submission.

Finalising and submitting your project

5

With much of the hard work on your project and presentation completed, there is still one last step. You need to understand the processes of evaluation and reflection, and apply the principles to your own learning.

Reflection is a requirement for EPQ assessment purposes: you must 'evaluate your own learning and performance', as outlined in the AO4 Review criteria[1] against which your work will be judged. At the same time, this evaluation and reflection process helps you to learn from the independent project process you have carried out. Independent learning is all about taking responsibility. It's up to you to reflect on what went well, and where you could do better. This allows you to build on the skills you may need in the future, and apply these in a range of situations.

This chapter will help you to:

- identify the criteria for evaluation, and define what we mean by reflection
- practise the processes of evaluation and reflection
- complete page 14 of your AQA Project Production Log & Assessment Record.

Keeping to a word limit is an important discipline to learn.

---

[1] © AQA 2007 Please refer to the current version of the specification on AQA's website at www.aqa.org.uk/over/extendedproject.php.

Chapter 5: Finalising and submitting your project

Evaluation and reflection

By the end of this section, you should be able to:
- carry out evaluation and reflection on the learning process and content of your project
- use evaluation and reflection as part of your learning process.

In order to evaluate your learning of the topic and processes involved in your project, you first need to consider the various stages you have carried out:
- choosing a topic
- researching your topic, including the resources you used and those you chose not to use; how you made use of ICT; the decision making, problem solving and critical thinking processes you were able to draw on
- writing up your report
- creating your artefact or product
- presenting your project.

When you evaluate these stages, you need to consider:
- what you learned about the topic
- pros and cons of the processes you used
- strengths and weaknesses of various techniques
- what went well and what didn't go so well.

Your reflections and evaluation will help you to learn from your experiences and approach similar tasks more effectively in the future.

> **Key terms**
>
> **Evaluation** to weigh up the good points and bad points of the content and learning process associated with your project with reference to the criteria for success
>
> **Reflection** to give something serious thought and consideration

What this means for my project

Your AQA Extended Project work will be judged against a set of Assessment Criteria[1] including:

AO4: Review

- Evaluate own learning and performance
- Convey and present evidenced outcomes and conclusions

This means that you will need to analyse the strengths and weaknesses of what you have learned and the processes you undertook. You also need to present evidence for why you arrived at these judgements.

ACTIVITY Reviewing your work

1. Go back through your Production Log and consider each stage of your project work. Consider these questions.

    - **What** skills have you learned?
    - **How** might you use these skills in the future, or in other areas of study?
    - **What** did you particularly enjoy about learning this topic?
    - **Were** there elements of this topic that you found less interesting?
    - **How** well do you think you carried out research, applied the research to your project, developed your artefact, and wrote and carried out your presentation? What went particularly well?
    - **What** could you have done better?
    - **What** would you do differently if you were to do this project again?
    - **What** piece of advice would you give a friend if they were going to do a similar project?

---

[1] © AQA 2007 Please refer to the current version of the specification on AQA's website at www.aqa.org.uk/over/extendedproject.php.

Completing your Project Production Log

By the end of this section, you should be able to:

- Explore some of the language you might use in the process of evaluation.
- Complete page 14 of your AQA Project Production Log & Assessment Record.

To complete page 14 of your AQA Project Production Log & Assessment Record, you need to discuss your learning and the processes involved in your project work. You should combine this with your judgement of your performance on these aspects of your project. You will need to:

- Provide evidence to support your judgements and conclusions
- Communicate your logic very clearly, using appropriate language
- Keep it relevant: only include information which you can back up with evidence
- Imagine your reader is an educated non-specialist.

ACTIVITY Evaluating and reporting on your work

1. Talk to a fellow student who is also producing an Extended Project. Discuss your reflections and thoughts on evaluating your project. Sometimes hearing someone else's ideas helps trigger a fresh way of looking at your own work.

2. Consider the language you could include in your Production Log.

   A Think about the language of conclusions, for example: what this means is ..., it is possible to conclude that ..., evidence shows that ..., it is clear that... What other ideas do you have?

   Think about the language of judgement. You may use a direct statement, such as 'this was fascinating' or 'this evidence was not backed up by other research'. You may use nouns such as 'In my view, ...' or 'In my opinion, ...'. You could compare and contrast the opinions of others that you have researched. What else?

   B When might it be appropriate to use 'must' or 'should'. For example: 'the next stage must be ...' or 'the team should look into the impact of their exhibition on ...'

Study tip

Remember that just because you feel or believe something does not put it beyond question. You need to be able to provide evidence of your opinion and back up your conclusions.

Links

Go to page 71 for more information on creative thinking, and how to encourage yourself to think about an issue with a fresh eye.

Chapter 5: Finalising and submitting your project

Checklist – are you ready for your project submission?

As part of the assessment evidence for your Extended Project at this stage in your work, you are required to:

- complete the AQA Project Production Log & Assessment Record
- sign the declaration on this form to confirm that the work is your own (other than where you have acknowledged the sources of information you have used, and the expected support that you have received)
- submit your final work.

Use this checklist to make sure you're appropriately prepared.[1]

Chapter 5: Finalising and submitting your project

	Comment on your next steps
The main points that I have learned about my project's topic are ...	
What I enjoyed about studying this topic is ...	
The aspects I thought were less interesting about this topic are ...	
The skills I have developed through this project are ...	
The skills I will use in the future, and the ways I will use these are ...	
The areas of my project that went really well are ...	
The areas of my performance that I could improve in the future are ...	
If I were to do this project again, the things I would do differently (and the reasons for these changes) are ...	
The advice I would give a friend if they were going to start on a project like this is ...	
My final proof reading of my report for inaccuracies and errors was important because ...	
The sort of changes I made in the quality of language in my report included ...	
I have completed page 14 of the AQA Project Production Log & Assessment Report	Yes No
What else do I need to do? ...	

---

[1] Filling in this chart is not an AQA requirement for EPQ. However it may help you to prepare for a meeting with your supervisor.

Project progress checkpoint

▶ 1 Project management skills: starting out

▶ 2 Project management skills: researching the project

▶ 3 Project management skills: producing the project product

▶ 4 Presenting your project

▼ 5 Finalising and submitting your project

Have you discussed the submission of your Project with your Supervisor?	Yes	No
Have you checked your report?	Yes	No
Have you completed page 14 of your AQA Project Production Log & Assessment Record?	Yes	No

Notes

Notes